Mix & Match MAMA

Meal Planner

SHAY SHULL

HARVEST HOUSE PUBLISHERS
EUGENE, OREGON

To Mom —

You never meal-planned but always

managed to deliver a spectacular supper.

xo

Cover design by Nicole Dougherty
Interior design by Faceout Studio
Food photos by Shay Shull
All other photos by Jay Eads

Published in association with William K. Jensen Literary Agency, 119 Bampton Court, Eugene, Oregon 97404

Mix and Match Mama® is a registered trademark of Mix and Match Mama, LLC

Mix-and-Match Mama® Meal Planner
Copyright © 2018 by Mix and Match Mama
Published by Harvest House Publishers
Eugene, Oregon 97408
www.harvesthousepublishers.com

ISBN 978-0-7369-7575-9 (softcover)
ISBN 978-0-7369-7576-6 (ebook)

Library of Congress Cataloging-in-Publication Data

Names: Shull, Shay, author.
Title: Mix-and-Match Mama meal planner / Shay Shull.
Other titles: Meal planner
Description: Eugene, Oregon: Harvest House Publishers, [2018] | Includes
   index.
Identifiers: LCCN 2018006348 (print) | LCCN 2018007169 (ebook) | ISBN
   9780736975766 (ebook) | ISBN 9780736975759 (pbk.)
Subjects: LCSH: Quick and easy cooking. | Seasonal cooking. | Menus. | LCGFT:
   Cookbooks.
Classification: LCC TX833.5 (ebook) | LCC TX833.5 .S534395 2018 (print) | DDC
   641.5/12--dc23
LC record available at https://lccn.loc.gov/2018006348

Printed in China

18 19 20 21 22 23 24 25 26 / RDS - FO / 10 9 8 7 6 5 4 3 2 1

Contents

Mix-and-Match Meal Planning

"What's for dinner?"

That famous phrase can make a woman's heart beat just a little faster. What's for dinner? What's for dinner? What *is* for dinner? Hmm...

Growing up, my mom put a hot meal on the table each and every night. It was always homemade, it was always delicious, and it was always spur-of-the-moment. My mom is famous for being in the middle of actually cooking our dinner (like ground beef was browning) and yet still not knowing what we were going to be having—a mere 15 minutes later! That is how my mom meal-planned. As she was cooking, she was planning.

Me? I need a very specific meal plan for the week. I need exact recipes, a solid grocery list, and a well-stocked pantry. I like to prepare everything in advance so that on busy nights I know exactly what to reach for and exactly what to prepare.

I need a meal plan.

When I introduced "Meal-Planning Mondays" to my blog readers, the feedback was very positive. From single gals to newlyweds, from busy moms with small kids to retired couples, everyone agreed: Cooking isn't hard; it's deciding what to make that can be challenging.

This weekly guide to getting dinner on the table is divided by seasons. Each season includes four weeks of recipes—seven dinners, plus one sweet treat per week.

Feel free to mix and match to fit your own life, though. You can make Mondays sandwich night and Fridays soup night if that works best. This is the fun and freedom of meal planning! And nothing is complicated—the recipes never have lengthy ingredient lists, uncommon spices, or take a long time to prepare.

Unless noted, all entrees in this book serve four.

Happy meal planning!

~Shay

Pantry Essentials

SEASONINGS
Chili powder
Cumin
Oregano
Italian seasoning
Pepper
Red pepper flakes
Salt
Taco seasoning
Worcestershire sauce

BAKING SUPPLIES
Baking soda
Flour
Sugar
Vanilla

OILS
Butter
Cooking spray
Extra virgin olive oil
Vegetable oil

CONDIMENTS
Ketchup
Mustard

Perfect Chicken

I call it my "Perfect Chicken." This is my biggest slow-cooker tip...poach your chicken in advance for a variety of meals. Simply place boneless, skinless chicken breasts in your slow cooker with enough water to cover them (about 6 cups or so). Put on the lid and cook on low for 6 to 8 hours or on high for 3 to 4 hours. That's it! The chicken will shred easily with just two forks. Discard the liquid.

Andrea's Pulled Pork

One of my very best friends, Andrea, gave me her amazing BBQ Pulled Pork recipe years ago, and it's a staple in our kitchen! Whenever you see Andrea's Pulled Pork in the book, refer to this recipe.

INGREDIENTS

1 (3 to 5 pounds) pork shoulder, pork butt, or pork tenderloin

1 large onion, chopped into big chunks

2 cans soda (not diet—I have used both Coca-Cola and Dr Pepper)

1 (12 to 18 ounce) bottle of your favorite BBQ Sauce (Andrea and I use Sweet Baby Ray's)

Place the pork and onion pieces in the bottom of the slow cooker. Pour the soda over the meat and onions, cover the slow cooker, and cook on high for at least 8 to 10 hours.

When you remove the lid after the cooking time, the meat should be falling apart at the touch of your fork. Remove all of the meat from the slow cooker into a bowl and then discard the onions and liquid. Add the meat back into the slow cooker and shred it with two forks. Stir in as much BBQ sauce as you like. At this point, you can serve immediately, or you can turn the slow cooker to the "keep warm" setting and let it stay warm for up to 4 or 5 hours until you're ready to eat.

Spring

Week 1 Meal Plan

MON	Tex-Mex Chicken Pot Pie
TUE	Hawaiian BBQ Chicken Burritos
WED	Sausage and Leek Pasta
THU	Spinach Calzones
FRI	Chicken Lettuce Wraps
SAT	Sweet Onion and Asparagus Pasta
SUN	Chicken Tortilla Soup Chick-fil-A Style
SWEET TREAT	Lemon Blueberry Cream Pie

Shopping List

PRODUCE
1 small onion
1 large sweet onion
10 to 12 green onions
3 leeks
6 scallions
1 green bell pepper
1 red bell pepper
1 jalapeño pepper
10 cloves garlic
8 to 10 basil leaves
2 cups baby portobello mushrooms
1 large handful chopped mushrooms (any variety)
10 (1 inch) pieces ginger root
10 oranges
10 heads of iceberg lettuce
10 to 12 asparagus spears
Parsley (garnish)
3 to 4 lemons
1 pint fresh blueberries

MEATS
2 pounds chicken
3 individual chicken breasts plus 2 pounds chicken breasts
2 pounds bulk Italian sausage (hot or sweet)
20 to 24 rounds turkey pepperoni

CANNED FOODS, CONDIMENTS, SOUPS, SAUCES
2 (10 ounce) cans Ro-Tel tomatoes
1 (6 ounce) can tomato paste
1 (8 ounce) jar sundried tomatoes in oil
4 1/2 cups chicken stock
1 1/2 cups chicken broth
1 cup BBQ sauce
1 (8 ounce) can crushed pineapple
1 (10 ounce) jar pizza sauce
1 (15 ounce) can black beans
1 (15 ounce) can Great Northern beans
1 (14.75 ounce) can creamed corn
1/2 cup hoisin sauce

GRAINS, PASTA, BREAD
1 (16 ounce) can refrigerated biscuits
1 (14 to 16 ounce) can or bag refrigerated pizza dough (or any pizza dough you love and have on hand)
5 burrito-sized tortillas
1 pound pasta (I use whole wheat rotini)
1 pound short-cut pasta (penne works well)
Tortilla chips (garnish)

FROZEN
2 cups frozen corn
1 (10 ounce) package frozen spinach

BAKING
1 (14 ounce) can sweetened condensed milk
1/4 cup powdered sugar
1 (3 ounce) package lemon instant pudding mix
1 premade graham cracker crust
2 tablespoons blueberry preserves or jam

DAIRY
1 cup Cheddar cheese, shredded
1 1/2 cups Parmesan cheese, grated
Shredded cheese (garnish—use your favorite kind for tortilla soup)
1 cup mozzarella or Italian-blend cheese
1 (8 ounce) package cream cheese
Milk
Half-and-half
Sour cream (garnish)
Whipped cream (garnish)

MON Tex-Mex Chicken Pot Pie

Really, is there anything more comforting than Chicken Pot Pie? I think not. I decided to *mix and match* it and make a Tex-Mex version. Yummy!

INGREDIENTS

1 pound Perfect Chicken (see page 6)

1 small onion, chopped

1 green bell pepper, chopped

1 jalapeño pepper, seeded and chopped (optional)

1 (10 ounce) can Ro-Tel tomatoes (do not drain)

1 (6 ounce) can tomato paste

1 tablespoon chili powder

1 cup chicken stock

1 cup frozen corn

1 can refrigerated biscuits

Salt and pepper

1 cup Cheddar cheese, shredded

Preheat oven to 425 degrees. Lightly spray an 8 x 8-inch baking dish with cooking spray; set aside. In a large skillet, combine the cooked chicken, onion, bell pepper, jalapeño pepper, Ro-Tel, tomato paste, chili powder, stock, and corn over medium-high heat. Add in a pinch of salt and pepper and bring to simmer for about 5 minutes.

After simmering, pour the chicken mixture into your prepared baking dish. Remove biscuits from the can and lay them across the top of mixture in the baking dish. Sprinkle a little cheese over the tops of each biscuit.

Bake for 8 to 10 minutes or until biscuits are brown and chicken mixture is bubbly. Remove from oven and serve. Everyone gets a scoop of Tex-Mex filling with a cheesy biscuit on top!

TUE Hawaiian BBQ Chicken Burritos

I'm really into the sweet and spicy flavors for spring. This little twist on a burrito takes the sweetness of pineapple and matches it with the spiciness of jalapeño. If you're serving your kiddos, you can just use a little less jalapeño. This is totally kid friendly!

INGREDIENTS

1 pound Perfect Chicken (see page 6)

1 cup BBQ sauce

1 jalapeño pepper, seeds removed and chopped (use less if you want less heat!)

1 (8 ounce) can crushed pineapple

8 to 10 green onions, chopped

5 burrito-sized tortillas

Preheat the oven to 375 degrees. In a mixing bowl, combine chicken, BBQ sauce, jalapeño pepper, pineapple, and green onions. Spoon chicken mixture down the center of each tortilla. Roll the tortillas burrito style by folding the ends down and then folding over each side.

Place the burritos seam side down on a foil-lined baking sheet that has been lightly greased. Bake 15 to 18 minutes or until lightly browned. You can drizzle a little extra pineapple, BBQ sauce, and/or green onions over each one before serving.

##

WED *Sausage and Leek Pasta*

Leeks are the perfect little sister to the onion, and they just make me happy. They're mild and so versatile, especially in a pasta dish. We used a bulk Italian pork sausage in this meal, but you can certainly substitute a chicken or turkey sausage.

INGREDIENTS

1 pound pasta (we use whole wheat rotini)

1 pound bulk Italian sausage, either hot or sweet

3 leeks, washed (see below) and chopped

3 cloves garlic, chopped

1½ cups chicken broth

1 (8 ounce) jar sundried tomatoes in oil, drained

½ cup Parmesan cheese, grated

8 to 10 basil leaves, torn or chopped

Extra virgin olive oil

Salt and pepper

Bring a large pot of water to boil, drop pasta in, and cook until al dente (7 to 8 minutes).

Meanwhile, over medium-high heat, heat a couple tablespoons of olive oil in a large pan. Once hot, add in sausage to brown (about 6 minutes). Let it brown without stirring it too often; drain. Add in leeks and garlic and sauté another 5 minutes. Add in chicken stock and lots of salt and pepper. Scrape up the little bits off the bottom of the pan, lower the heat to medium-low, and simmer 3 to 5 minutes. Stir in tomatoes.

Drain pasta and add to sausage mixture. Stir in cheese and basil.

Note: Leeks are grown in sandy soil, so you can't just wash the outsides; you have to wash the insides too. The easiest way is to chop the leeks, place them in a colander in your sink, and then run lots of cold water over the tops. Use a paper towel to lightly pat them dry.

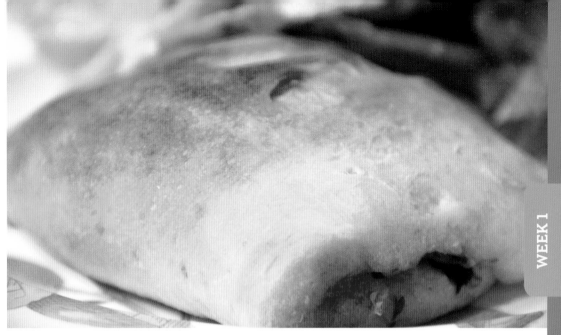

THU
Spinach Calzones

You can buy the ingredients for this versatile recipe way in advance and keep them in your fridge for last-minute meals. These calzones take no time to prepare, and you can mix and match a million ways. If your family doesn't love spinach, leave it out. If you prefer browned sausage, go for it! If you would rather throw in a ton of chopped veggies with no meat, be my guest!

INGREDIENTS

Drizzles of extra virgin olive oil

1 box frozen spinach, thawed and drained of excess water

3 cloves garlic, chopped

1 (10 ounce) jar pizza sauce

1 can refrigerated pizza dough (or any pizza dough you love and have on hand)

Turkey pepperoni (or whatever meat you like)

1 cup mozzarella or Italian blend cheese

Preheat the oven to 425 degrees.

Line a baking sheet with foil and spray with cooking spray for easy cleanup.

In a small skillet, heat a drizzle of olive oil over medium heat. Add the spinach and stir for 2 to 3 minutes. Add the garlic and cook for another minute. Remove from heat. (You're just getting the spinach warm and infused with the garlic.)

Spread the dough into a rectangle and cut into four squares. On one half of each square, put 2 tablespoons pizza sauce. Then layer 5 to 6 pepperoni, 2 tablespoons or so of the spinach mixture, and a few tablespoons of cheese. Fold the other half of the square on top. Press the sides down to seal in all the filling. Cut two little slits across the top of each calzone with a knife. Then brush each with a drizzle of oil. Bake for 9 to 10 minutes or until the dough is golden brown.

FRI Chicken Lettuce Wraps

Lettuce wraps are my favorite. They're light and crunchy and oh so yummy. And they're perfect paired with a warm spring evening.

INGREDIENTS

2 tablespoons vegetable oil

3 chicken breasts, chopped into bite-sized pieces

2 cups baby portobello mushrooms

Salt and pepper

4 cloves garlic, chopped

1-inch piece ginger, grated or finely chopped (substitute one teaspoon ground ginger)

Zest of one orange

1 red bell pepper, chopped

6 scallions, chopped

½ cup hoisin sauce (Chinese BBQ sauce; find in the international foods aisle)

1 head iceberg lettuce, leaves separated

Preheat a skillet to high heat. Add the oil to the hot pan. Add the chicken pieces to the pan and stir-fry a couple of minutes. Add the mushrooms and cook another couple of minutes. Season with salt and pepper after the mushrooms have browned (not before!). Add the garlic and ginger. Cook another minute, and then add the orange zest, bell pepper, and scallions, stirring to combine well. Cook another minute. Add the hoisin sauce, coating everything evenly.

Serve the chicken mixture inside the lettuce leaves.

SAT # Sweet Onion and Asparagus Pasta

Spring is the time for adding seasonal ingredients to your meals—like sweet onion, asparagus, and mushrooms...yum! The beauty of this little method is that you can sub any veggies that look good to you (bell pepper, zucchini, cherry tomatoes...whatever). I use sweet Italian chicken sausage in my pasta, but any sausage will work (pork, chicken, or turkey).

INGREDIENTS

1 pound short-cut pasta (penne works well)

1 to 2 tablespoons extra virgin olive oil

1 pound sausage

1 large sweet onion, chopped

1 clove garlic, chopped

A large handful of mushrooms (any variety), chopped

2 cups chicken stock

1 cup grated Parmesan cheese, divided

10 to 12 asparagus stalks, chopped into bite-sized pieces

A splash of milk, cream, or half-and-half

Salt and pepper

Parsley for garnish

Bring a large pot of water to a boil over medium-high heat. Drop in the pasta and cook to al dente (6 minutes or so).

Meanwhile, in a large skillet over medium-high heat, drizzle a tablespoon or so of olive oil. Add the sausage and brown.

Once the sausage is browned and crumbly, add the onion and sauté a few minutes until soft. Add the garlic and mushrooms. Sauté a few more minutes. Stir in the chicken stock and deglaze your pan (scrape the little bits off the bottom). Stir in a $\frac{1}{2}$ cup of the Parmesan cheese and the asparagus, reduce the heat to low, and simmer for 5 minutes. Stir in the milk, cream, or half-and-half and a pinch of salt and pepper. Drain the pasta and add to the skillet of sausage. Stir to incorporate.

Garnish with parsley and the remaining Parmesan cheese.

Chicken Tortilla Soup Chick-fil-A Style

Usually when I take the kids to Chick-Fil-A, I don't eat anything...I bring a latte and then eat when I get home. But after my daughter raved about this soup, a sweet gal sent me this recipe. I made it...I loved it. This might just be my favorite version of Chicken Tortilla Soup. (Plus I made it a slow cooker version...even better!)

INGREDIENTS

1 pound chicken breast (thawed or frozen)

1 (15 ounce) can black beans

1 (15 ounce) can Great Northern beans

1 (10 ounce) can Ro-Tel tomatoes

1½ cups chicken stock

1 packet taco seasoning

1 (14.75 ounce) can creamed corn

1 cup frozen corn kernels

¾ cup half-and-half

Green onion for garnish, chopped

Sour cream for garnish

Cheese for garnish, shredded

Tortilla chips

In a slow cooker, add the chicken, black beans, Great Northern beans, tomatoes, chicken stock, and taco seasoning. Cook on low for 6 hours or on high for 3 hours.

Remove the lid and shred the chicken inside the slow cooker using two forks. Stir in the creamed corn and frozen corn kernels and, keeping the lid off, cook another 20 minutes on high. (This will allow some of the liquid to evaporate and give you a thicker soup.) Just before you're ready to serve, stir in the half-and-half. Ladle the soup into bowls and garnish with the toppings. Serve with tortilla chips.

SWEET TREAT · Lemon Blueberry Cream Pie

My cousin Brooke gave me this simple recipe, and it is the perfect dessert to make with kids. No oven, no knives, just yummy goodness.

INGREDIENTS

1 (8 ounce) package cream cheese, softened

1 (14 ounce) can sweetened condensed milk

¼ cup powdered sugar

2 teaspoons lemon zest

½ cup fresh lemon juice

1 (3 ounce) package lemon instant pudding mix (do not prepare—you just need the powder)

1 premade graham cracker crust

1 pint fresh blueberries

2 tablespoons blueberry preserves or jam

Whipped cream to garnish

In a large mixing bowl, beat cream cheese, milk, and powdered sugar with an electric mixer until creamy. Beat in lemon pudding mix, lemon zest, and lemon juice until just blended. Pour half of lemon mixture into prepared pie crust.

Stir together fresh blueberries with blueberry preserves in a small bowl. Pour the blueberry mixture evenly over the top of the lemon pie layer. Top the blueberry layer with the other half of the lemon mixture. Chill the pie at least two hours (you can even chill it overnight!). Remove the pie from fridge and cut into wedges. Serve with a garnish of whipped cream.

Week 2 Meal Plan

MON	Chicken Florentine Enchiladas
TUE	Spicy Chicken Baked Tacos
WED	Mushroom Sausage Kale Pasta
THU	Coconut-Crusted Chicken
FRI	Jolly Green Joes
SAT	Spring Vegetable Risotto
SUN	Chicken and Wild Rice Soup
SWEET TREAT	Vanilla Bean Poppy Seed Cupcakes

Shopping List

PRODUCE

1 green bell pepper
1 red bell pepper
1 red onion
1 yellow onion
8 to 10 green onions
4 leeks
1 jalapeño pepper
1 shallot
4 cups kale
2 zucchinis
10 asparagus stalks
6 to 9 cloves garlic
1 avocado
2 pints sliced mushrooms (any variety)
2 cups chopped carrots or baby carrots
Parsley (garnish)

MEATS

2 pounds chicken
2 pounds chicken breast
1 pound Italian sausage
   (turkey, chicken, or pork)
2 cups chicken, cooked and chopped (optional)
1 pound ground turkey

CANNED FOODS, CONDIMENTS, SOUPS, SAUCES

1 (10.5 ounce) can cream of chicken soup
1 (10 ounce) can enchilada sauce
1 (4 ounce) can chopped green chilies
2 cups salsa
1½ cups green chili or tomatillo salsa
4 quarts chicken stock
3 tablespoons poultry seasoning
2 bay leaves
Orange marmalade (garnish)

GRAINS, PASTA, BREAD

8 tortillas (either flour or whole wheat)
6 to 8 taco shells
1 pound pasta (we use penne)
1 cup Arborio rice
1 (6 ounce) box wild rice (unprepared)
Burger buns (enough to feed your family)

FROZEN

2 (10 ounce) packages frozen spinach
1 cup frozen peas

BAKING

Bisquick
1½ cups shredded sweetened coconut
2 cups powdered sugar
1 vanilla bean
4 teaspoons poppy seeds

DAIRY

1 cup shredded Monterey Jack cheese
2 cups shredded Pepper Jack cheese
1½ cups grated Parmesan cheese
   (plus extra for garnish)
Half-and-half
Milk
Eggs
1 (8 ounce) container sour cream

MON *Chicken Florentine Enchiladas*

We love making enchiladas at our house. They always look a little fancy, but they're a really simple weeknight supper. Honestly, this yummy meal can be on your table in less than 30 minutes. From my table to yours, enjoy!

INGREDIENTS

1 pound Perfect Chicken (see page 6)

1 (10 ounce) package frozen spinach, thawed and excess water squeezed out

1 red bell pepper, chopped and divided

1 red onion, chopped

1 can cream of chicken soup

2 teaspoons cumin (use chili powder if you don't have cumin)

Salt and pepper

1 cup Monterey Jack cheese, shredded

8 tortillas (either flour or whole wheat)

1 (10 ounce) can enchilada sauce

Preheat oven to 400 degrees. Lightly spray an 8 x 8-inch baking dish with cooking spray; set aside. In a large mixing bowl, combine shredded chicken with spinach, bell pepper, half of the onion, cream of chicken soup, cumin, a pinch of salt and pepper, and cheese. Once combined, spread a little bit down the center of each tortilla. Roll and place in the prepared baking dish. Once all 8 enchiladas are tucked inside the baking dish, pour enchilada sauce on top of them.

Bake uncovered about 20 minutes or until the edges of the tortillas are lightly brown and everything is bubbling. Remove from oven and sprinkle the remaining red onion over the top.

TUE

Spicy Chicken Baked Tacos

Simple and delicious—perfect for a busy weeknight! You should totally try it. Tonight.

INGREDIENTS

1 pound Perfect Chicken (see page 6)

1 jalapeño pepper, chopped (remove the seeds for less heat)

1 package taco seasoning

1 (10 ounce) package frozen spinach, thawed and excess water squeezed out

2 cups salsa

Extra virgin olive oil

6 to 8 taco shells

2 cups shredded Pepper Jack cheese

Preheat oven to 425 degrees. In a large skillet over medium-high heat, combine cooked chicken, jalapeño pepper, taco seasoning, spinach, and salsa in a tablespoon or so of olive oil. Reduce the heat to low and simmer about 5 minutes.

Meanwhile, in an 8 x 8-inch baking dish sprayed with cooking spray, line up taco shells. Divide the chicken mixture between the shells. Top tacos with cheese and pop dish in the oven. Bake about 10 minutes or until the cheese is bubbly and brown.

Mushroom Sausage Kale Pasta

My family loves pasta for supper, and I love making pasta like this for my kiddos because they eat it up...kale and all. If you're not into kale, feel free to substitute fresh spinach instead. Just mix and match it for your family!

INGREDIENTS

1 pound Italian sausage (turkey, chicken, or pork)

1 pound pasta (we use penne)

1 shallot, chopped

2 cups chopped mushrooms (any variety you like)

4 cups kale, torn into bite-sized pieces (just a few big handfuls)

1 cup chicken stock

Extra virgin olive oil

1 cup Parmesan cheese, grated

Splash of half-and-half, whipping cream, or milk

Salt and pepper

In a large skillet over medium-high heat, drizzle in just a tablespoon or so of olive oil. Add sausage (if it's in the casing, remove from casing first) and begin to brown.

On a second burner, bring a large pot of water to boil for the pasta. Drop in pasta and cook to al dente.

Once the sausage is browned and crumbly, drain off fat and then add in chopped shallot and sauté just a minute or so. Add in chopped mushrooms and kale. Stir in the stock and deglaze the pan (scrape up the little bits off of the bottom of the pan). Reduce heat to medium and allow mixture to bubble a few minutes.

Drain pasta and add to the sausage mixture. Stir in Parmesan cheese and a splash of half-and-half. Add just a pinch of salt and pepper and serve (maybe with a bit more Parmesan to garnish).

THU Coconut-Crusted Chicken

Spooning a little marmalade over the top takes things to a whole new level. Serve it with green beans for a quick and easy weeknight meal!

INGREDIENTS

¾ cup Bisquick mix

1½ cups sweetened coconut, shredded

Salt and pepper

1 egg, beaten

1 pound chicken breasts

2 tablespoons butter, melted

Orange marmalade for garnish

Preheat oven to 400 degrees. In one shallow dish (such as a pie plate), combine Bisquick, coconut, and a pinch of salt and pepper. In a second shallow dish, beat the egg. Dip each chicken breast first in the beaten egg, coating well on both sides, and then in the Bisquick mixture.

Place chicken on greased, foil-lined baking sheet. Brush half the melted butter over the tops of the chicken and bake 8 minutes. Flip chicken over and brush remaining half of the melted butter on the opposite side and cook another 8 minutes. The chicken should be brown and crispy with the juices running clear. Remove chicken from oven and garnish with a little orange marmalade on top.

Jolly Green Joes

The Jolly Green Joe was born when I was trying to think of a sloppy joe I could serve on St. Patrick's Day. Ground turkey plus spinach, green bell pepper, green chilies, green onions, avocado—all jolly and green and perfect for St. Paddy's Day (or any old night, for that matter!).

INGREDIENTS

1 pound ground turkey

Extra virgin olive oil

Salt and pepper

1 (10 ounce) package frozen spinach, thawed and drained of excess water

1 green bell pepper, chopped

1 (4 ounce) can chopped green chilies

1½ cups green chili or tomatillo salsa

8 to 10 green onions, chopped

Burger buns

1 avocado, pit removed and sliced into pieces

In a large skillet over medium-high heat, brown the turkey in a drizzle of olive oil until browned and crumbly. Add a liberal pinch of salt and pepper. Stir in the spinach, bell pepper, green chilies, salsa, and onions (saving a few to garnish). Reduce the heat to medium and let the mixture simmer for about 5 minutes or until everything is heated through.

Top each burger bun with a generous portion of ground turkey mixture. Garnish with pieces of avocado and a few remaining chopped green onions.

SAT ## Spring Vegetable Risotto

In spring, the food needs to be fresh, light, and simple. This is a nice side dish with a piece of fish or steak. However, I love chicken in the risotto. Try my Perfect Chicken method (see page 6).

INGREDIENTS

2 quarts chicken stock (or veggie stock if you're making this a vegetarian dish)

1 tablespoon butter

1 tablespoon extra virgin olive oil

2 zucchini, chopped

10 asparagus stalks, chopped

1 onion, chopped

3 to 6 cloves garlic, chopped

1 cup Arborio rice

1 cup frozen peas

2 cups chicken, chopped and cooked (optional)

$\frac{1}{2}$ cup Parmesan cheese, grated

Salt and pepper

In a large stockpot, bring chicken stock to low simmer (not boiling). In a separate pan, melt butter with 1 tablespoon olive oil over medium-high heat. Add in zucchini and asparagus and sauté 4 to 5 minutes. Remove veggies from pan, cover, and set aside. Add onion and garlic to skillet and cook 4 to 5 minutes. Stir in rice for another minute.

At this point, take a ladle and add 1 cup of the hot stock to the rice. Stir constantly for a minute or so. As the liquid evaporates, the rice will become super starchy and delicious. Stir pretty often, adding stock every time the majority of the liquid evaporates. You will continue doing this for about 18 minutes. Add stock, stir, wait for it to evaporate, and add more. This will cause the risotto to fluff up and look creamy (without using any cream!). A lot of recipes will tell you to stir continuously, but you don't need to. Just stir it every few minutes and you'll be fine.

After the rice is tender (take a bite!), stir in frozen peas, zucchini, asparagus, and chicken and continue cooking another 3 to 4 minutes. Stir in cheese; season with lots of salt and pepper to taste.

Chicken and Wild Rice Soup

What's better on a cool spring evening than chicken soup? Feel free to mix and match the seasonal ingredients according to what's fresh in your garden, at the farm stand, or in the grocery store.

INGREDIENTS

Extra virgin olive oil

4 leeks, cleaned and chopped

3 cloves garlic, chopped

1 pint mushrooms, sliced (whatever kind you love)

2 cups carrots or baby carrots, chopped

1 pound chicken, cooked and shredded

3 tablespoons poultry seasoning

2 bay leaves (dried or fresh)

Salt and pepper

1 (32 ounce) box of chicken stock

1 (6 ounce) box of wild rice (unprepared)

$\frac{1}{4}$ cup cream or milk (whichever you have)

Parmesan cheese for garnish, grated (optional)

Parsley for garnish, chopped (optional)

In a large pot over medium-high heat, pour a big drizzle of olive oil along with your chopped (and cleaned, see note on page 12) leeks. Allow the leeks to sauté until tender (5 to 8 minutes). After that, stir in the garlic and sauté for a minute. Next, add the mushrooms and carrots and continue sautéing 3 or 4 more minutes. Then add the chicken, followed by the poultry seasoning, bay leaves, and a big pinch of salt and pepper. Slowly stir in the chicken stock and uncooked wild rice. Bring everything to a boil, and as soon as it boils, reduce the heat to a simmer and continue simmering uncovered for 20 minutes (stirring often).

After about 20 minutes, the veggies should be tender and the rice should be cooked. At this point, stir in the cream or milk. Turn off the heat and ladle into bowls and garnish with a bit of grated Parmesan cheese and chopped parsley. (Don't forget to remove the bay leaves before serving.)

SWEET TREAT

Vanilla Bean Poppy Seed Cupcakes

I love anything vanilla bean and anything with poppy seeds! Together they make one delicious cupcake.

INGREDIENTS

1³/₄ cups flour

1³/₄ cups sugar

1 teaspoon baking soda

¹/₂ teaspoon salt

2 eggs

²/₃ cup butter, softened, plus another ¹/₂ cup butter, softened

1 (8 ounce) container sour cream

1 vanilla bean, split down the center

4 teaspoons poppy seeds, divided

2 cups powdered sugar

1 tablespoon milk

Preheat the oven to 350 degrees. Line 1 (12 count) muffin tin with cupcake liners and then a second muffin tin halfway full of liners (yields about 18 cupcakes). Set aside.

In a large mixing bowl, combine flour, sugar, baking soda, and salt with a whisk. Set aside.

In a second mixing bowl, beat with an electric mixer ²/₃ cup softened butter with the sour cream and eggs. Slowly beat the flour mixture into this bowl. Once incorporated, beat in half of the seeds from vanilla bean (reserve the other half for the frosting) and 2 teaspoons of poppy seeds.

Pour batter into prepared cupcake liners (batter will be nice and thick) and bake 18 to 20 minutes or until a toothpick inserted into the center of one cupcake comes out clean.

Allow cupcakes to cool completely before frosting.

To make the frosting, beat ¹/₂ cup softened butter with powdered sugar and milk. Once frosting reaches desired consistency, beat in the other half of the seeds from your vanilla bean and two teaspoons of poppy seeds. Frost cooled cupcakes. Store in the fridge when you're not enjoying.

Week 3 Meal Plan

MON	Teriyaki Chicken in the Slow Cooker
TUE	BBQ Pork Rice Bowls
WED	Shrimp Caprese Pasta
THU	Pulled Pork Stuffed Potatoes
FRI	Cheeseburger Meatballs
SAT	Lemon Pesto Salmon
SUN	Italian Wedding Soup
SWEET TREAT	Lemon Coconut Bars

Shopping List

PRODUCE

22 to 24 green onions
4 large onions
1 red onion
1 cup corn kernels (can use frozen)
2 avocados
1 pint cherry tomatoes
1½ cups basil leaves
1 cup cilantro leaves (plus extra for garnish)
4 to 6 large russet potatoes
2 garlic cloves
2 lemons
Parsley (garnish)

MEATS

1 pound boneless, skinless chicken breasts
2 (6 to 10 pounds) pork shoulders, pork butts,
   or pork tenderloins
1 pound peeled and deveined shrimp
   (fresh or frozen)
1 large piece of fish, divided into 4 pieces or 4
   separate fillets (I use sockeye salmon)
1 pound ground beef
1 (1 pound) bag frozen meatballs

CANNED FOODS, CONDIMENTS, SOUPS, SAUCES

1 cup soy sauce
Rice wine vinegar (or apple cider vinegar)
Honey
1 cup chicken stock
4 cups beef stock
4 cans soda (not diet—I use both Coca-Cola
   and Dr Pepper)
3 (18 ounce) bottles of your favorite BBQ sauce
   (I like Sweet Baby Ray's)
1 (1 ounce) packet dry ranch dressing mix
Relish (garnish)
2 teaspoons garlic powder

1 (15 ounce) can tomato sauce
1 (14 ounce) can diced tomatoes
1 (28 ounce) can tomatoes (I love San Marzano)

GRAINS, PASTA, BREAD

3 cups cooked white rice
4 cups cooked brown rice
4 cups wild rice, cooked
1 pound pasta (I use whole wheat rotini)
1 box (about 4 cups) small pasta
Sesame seeds (garnish)
1 cup slivered almonds

FROZEN

1 (10 ounce) package frozen spinach
1 (10 ounce) package frozen carrots

BAKING

2 tablespoons cornstarch
½ cup breadcrumbs or panko breadcrumbs
1 (15.25 ounce) box lemon cake mix
1 box powdered sugar (about 4 cups)
2 cups sweetened flaked coconut

DAIRY

Fresh mozzarella cheese (garnish)
3 cups shredded Cheddar cheese
1 cup Parmesan cheese (plus extra for garnish)
6 eggs
1 (8 ounce) package cream cheese
2 (8 ounce) containers sour cream

MON # Teriyaki Chicken in the Slow Cooker

One-pot meals keep things super simple. Get dinner going ahead of time in a slow cooker, and then whip up a batch of rice and ladle the chicken on top. A very quick, very yummy slow-cooker supper.

INGREDIENTS

1 pound boneless, skinless chicken breasts

1 cup soy sauce

¼ cup rice wine vinegar (or feel free to use apple cider vinegar)

¼ cup honey (just a big squeeze of it!)

1 cup chicken stock

2 tablespoons water

2 tablespoons cornstarch

3 cups cooked and ready-to-eat white rice

Sesame seeds for garnish, toasted (optional)

Green onions for garnish, chopped (optional)

In a slow cooker, add the chicken, soy sauce, vinegar, honey, and stock. Cover and cook on low for 6 to 8 hours or on high for 3 hours. About 30 minutes before you're ready to eat, remove the lid and shred the chicken inside the slow cooker, using two forks. Then, in a small bowl, whisk together the water and cornstarch and quickly whisk that mixture into the slow cooker. Cover and cook on high for the last 20 or 30 minutes.

When you're ready to serve, ladle the chicken on top of the cooked rice. Garnish with toasted sesame seeds (add a big handful to a clean, dry skillet and toast them over medium-high heat...it will only take 2 to 3 minutes!) and some chopped green onions.

 **TUE** *BBQ Pork Rice Bowls*

We love rice bowls around our house. Everyone fills their bowl with their favorite toppings, and then we sit down to a cozy dinner. Rice, pulled pork, some creamy avocado, and corn. Dinner is done!

INGREDIENTS

1 pound Andrea's Pulled Pork (see page 6)

1 cup cooked corn kernels, warm or at room temperature (not frozen)

2 avocados, peeled and diced

8 green onions, chopped

4 cups rice, cooked and ready to eat (we use brown rice)

Place the pulled pork in a large mixing bowl and stir in the corn.

Take each serving bowl and add about a cup of rice to each one. Top the rice with the BBQ pork and corn mixture. Then top everything with avocado and green onions.

Shrimp Caprese Pasta

I combined three of our family's favorite things into one dish: pasta, shrimp, and a Caprese salad. My *favorite* thing about this recipe, though? It comes together in *minutes*! Plus, all the kiddos (and the adults) are huge fans...that's what you call a winning situation.

INGREDIENTS

1 pint cherry tomatoes

Extra virgin olive oil

Salt and pepper

1 pound pasta (we use whole wheat rotini)

1 red onion, chopped

1 (28 ounce) can tomatoes (I love San Marzano)

1 pound shrimp, peeled and deveined (if you use frozen, make sure to bring them to room temp first, per package directions)

Fresh mozzarella cheese for garnish, cut into pieces

Fresh basil for garnish, torn into pieces

Preheat the oven to 400 degrees. Line a baking sheet with foil (for easy cleanup).

Place the cherry tomatoes on the baking sheet. Drizzle olive oil over the tomatoes along with a big pinch of salt and pepper. Pop your tomatoes into the oven and roast for 15 minutes.

Bring a pot of water to a boil and drop the pasta inside. Cook to al dente (7 or 8 minutes).

Meanwhile, in a large skillet over medium-high heat, add the red onion with a drizzle of olive oil, and pinch of salt and pepper. Sauté until tender and then add the canned tomatoes. Using a wooden spoon, lightly break up the tomatoes as they cook together with the onion. Remove roasted cherry tomatoes from the oven and add them to the skillet too. Next, stir in the shrimp along with another pinch of salt and pepper. The shrimp will heat up in about 3 minutes.

Drain the pasta water, add the hot pasta to skillet, and then toss everything together. Ladle the pasta onto plates and garnish with fresh mozzarella and torn basil.

THU Pulled Pork Stuffed Potatoes

We love Andrea's Pulled Pork recipe and make it a lot at our house (especially on busy nights). The other evening I made a batch and decided to stuff potatoes with it instead of eating it sandwich-style...and you know what? I think I loved it even more!

INGREDIENTS

1 (1 ounce) packet dry ranch dressing mix (do not prepare)

1 (8 ounce) container sour cream

1 cup BBQ sauce (we use Sweet Baby Ray's)

4 to 6 large russet potatoes, baked and ready to eat

1 batch Andrea's Pulled Pork (see page 6)

2 cups Cheddar cheese, shredded

10 green onions, chopped

In a small bowl, stir together half of the ranch dressing mix (you'll only need half), sour cream, and BBQ sauce. After everything is incorporated, set aside.

Cut open each of the baked potatoes and fluff up the inside a bit. Next, place a big dollop of the sour cream mixture inside each potato, followed by a generous portion of Andrea's Pulled Pork. Toss everything together within each potato and then top with shredded Cheddar and chopped green onions.

FRI Cheeseburger Meatballs

You guys probably know I'm meatball obsessed. Well, I'm also cheeseburger obsessed. So I turned meatballs into cheeseburgers. All the flavor but without the grill!

INGREDIENTS

1 pound ground beef

½ cup breadcrumbs or panko

1 cup Cheddar cheese, shredded

2 eggs, beaten

1 onion, finely chopped

Generous pinches salt and pepper

4 tablespoons Worcestershire sauce, divided

1½ cups ketchup

2 teaspoons mustard

Relish to garnish

Preheat oven to 425 degrees. Mix ground beef, breadcrumbs, cheese, eggs, onion, salt, pepper, and 2 tablespoons Worcestershire sauce in a bowl. Form into meatballs and line them up on a greased, foil-lined baking sheet.

Next, combine remaining 2 tablespoons Worcestershire sauce, ketchup, and mustard in a bowl. Top each meatball with sauce and bake 15-18 minutes, or until they're browned and cooked through. Garnish with a little relish.

SAT Lemon Pesto Salmon

We make pesto all the time at our house and are constantly mixing and matching it. This version has cilantro, basil, and lemon zest in it...so much flavor in one little topping.

INGREDIENTS

1 cup cilantro leaves (loosely packed, not chopped)

1 cup basil leaves (loosely packed, not chopped)

1 cup toasted almonds (just toast them in a clean, dry skillet for about 3 minutes)

2 cloves garlic

1 cup Parmesan cheese, grated

Zest of one lemon (plus a bit more for garnish)

½ to 1 cup extra virgin olive oil (plus a bit more for the fish)

4 fish fillets (we use sockeye salmon)

Salt and pepper

Brown and/or wild rice (optional)

Preheat the oven to 400 degrees. Line a baking sheet with foil and lightly coat with cooking spray (for easy cleanup). Set aside.

Place the first six ingredients in the bowl of a food processor. Cover and turn on to mix the ingredients. Slowly pour the olive oil into the food processor, and you'll see the pesto begin to form. Slowly keep adding olive oil until the pesto reaches a desired consistency. Because this is a garnish on top of the fish, I prefer my pesto to be thicker rather than thinner. Stop the food processor when you think it's ready to go. Scrape the pesto into a bowl and reserve.

Meanwhile, take the fish and pour a bit of olive oil on top along with a nice sprinkle of both salt and pepper. Place the fish on the prepared baking sheet and pop in the oven for 2 to 15 minutes (depending on how well done you like it).

When the fish has finished cooking, remove from the oven and serve over a bed of rice. Top the fish with the pesto, and then add a garnish of lemon zest to complete.

SUN	

Italian Wedding Soup

This is my easy weeknight spin on a classic. So much goodness in every bowl.

INGREDIENTS

1 (1 pound) bag frozen meatballs

1 onion, chopped

4 cups beef stock

2 teaspoons garlic powder

1 (15 ounce) can tomato sauce

1 (14 ounce) can diced tomatoes

1 (10 ounce) package frozen spinach, thawed and drained of excess water

1 (10 ounce) package frozen carrots

1 box (about 4 cups or so) small pasta

Parmesan cheese for garnish, grated

Cilantro or parsley for garnish, chopped

In the slow cooker, mix together the meatballs, onion, beef stock, garlic powder, tomato sauce, and diced tomatoes. Cover and cook on low for 6 to 7 hours or on high for 3 to 4 hours. About 20 minutes before you're ready to eat, stir in the spinach, carrots, and pasta. Cover and turn the slow cooker to high for the last 20 minutes. When you're ready to serve, ladle the soup into bowls and garnish with Parmesan cheese and either a little cilantro or parsley.

SWEET TREAT *Lemon Coconut Bars*

This is it! This is the bar you will make over and over again this spring and summer. You'll make it once, everyone will love it, and then you'll keep making it for every occasion between now and Labor Day. This is your new favorite bar.

INGREDIENTS

1 box lemon cake mix

4 eggs, divided

1 stick melted butter

1 box powdered sugar (about 4 cups)

1 (8 ounce) package cream cheese, softened

2 cups sweetened flaked coconut

Preheat oven to 350 degrees. Grease one 9 x 13-inch baking pan.

In a mixing bowl, combine cake mix, 2 eggs, and melted butter. Spread in bottom of pan.

In a second bowl, beat with electric mixer powdered sugar, 2 more eggs, and cream cheese. Stir in coconut. Spread coconut mixture on top of crust mixture.

Bake 35 to 40 minutes until edges are brown and the center is set (it will still be slightly wobbly in the middle).

Cool on counter 30 minutes, then refrigerate 2 hours or up to 2 days. Slice into bars and serve.

Week 4 Meal Plan

MON	Chicken Cacciatore in the Slow Cooker
TUE	Teriyaki Chicken Wraps
WED	Spinach Pesto Pasta Bake
THU	Pesto Meatballs
FRI	Ham and Swiss with Pesto Sandwiches
SAT	Bacon and Broccoli Quinoa
SUN	Margarita Chicken Soup
SWEET TREAT	Strawberry Shortcake Trifle

Shopping List

PRODUCE

1 onion
1 red onion
6 to 8 green onions
2 shallots
9 to 10 cloves garlic
2 red bell peppers
1 green bell pepper
1 to 2 bell peppers, any color (optional for sandwiches)
1 (8 ounce) package mushrooms (I use cremini)
Cilantro (garnish)
2 cups broccoli florets
Spinach (optional for sandwiches)
1 to 2 cucumbers (optional for sandwiches)
2 limes
1 avocado
1 pint fresh strawberries

MEATS

2 pounds boneless, skinless chicken breasts
1 pound chicken
2 pounds ground beef
8 pieces bacon (I use turkey bacon)
Sliced ham (for however many sandwiches you are making)

CANNED FOODS, CONDIMENTS, SOUPS, SAUCES

1½ cups dry white wine
1 cup chicken stock
1 (8 ounce) can pineapple pieces
½ cup teriyaki sauce
2 (7 ounce) jars pesto
Spaghetti sauce for dipping or drizzling (optional)
1 (10 ounce) can Ro-Tel tomatoes
1 (12 ounce) can Sprite or 7-Up (can be diet)
1 (15 ounce) can black beans
1 (14 ounce) can diced tomatoes
1 (28 ounce) can whole tomatoes (I love San Marzano)
1 (14 ounce) can creamed corn

GRAINS, PASTA, BREAD

1 pound egg noodles
1 pound pasta (any kind)
2 cups quinoa
4 flour tortillas
2 slices of bread (or an English muffin or whatever you like) per person

FROZEN

3 (10 ounce) packages frozen spinach

BAKING

1 cup breadcrumbs or panko breadcrumbs
1 (5 ounce) package instant vanilla pudding
1 (14 ounce) can sweetened condensed milk
1 pound cake

DAIRY

1 (3 ounce) package cream cheese
1 cup shredded mozzarella cheese
1½ cups shredded Cheddar cheese (plus extra for garnish)
Swiss cheese (enough for sandwiches)
1 cup grated Parmesan cheese (plus extra for garnish)
2 eggs
5 cups milk (plus a little extra)
1 (12 ounce) container Cool Whip

MON Chicken Cacciatore in the Slow Cooker

This dish is a quintessential slow cooker supper...you put almost everything in before you head out the door in the morning, come home, boil some pasta, and BAM! Dinner is done. Easy as that. This super simple slow cooker supper makes it easy to sit down and enjoy a home-cooked meal with your family even on the busiest of nights.

INGREDIENTS

1 pound boneless, skinless chicken breasts

1 onion, chopped

3 cloves garlic, chopped

1 red bell pepper, chopped

1 green bell pepper, chopped

1 (8 ounce) package mushrooms (I use cremini)

1 (28 ounce) can whole tomatoes
 (I love San Marzano)

1½ cups dry white wine

1 cup chicken stock (or water)

Salt and pepper to taste

1 pound egg noodles, cooked to al dente
 (or whatever pasta you have on hand)

Parmesan cheese for garnish, grated

Add the first 7 ingredients to your slow cooker. Next, pour the wine and stock over everything. (If you don't want to use wine, you can just substitute with more stock). Add a big pinch of salt and pepper. Cover and cook on low for 7 to 9 hours or on high for 3 to 4 hours.

When you're ready to serve, remove the lid and shred the chicken inside the slow cooker, using two forks. Also, slightly mash the whole tomatoes. To serve, add cooked egg noodles to a bowl and then top with a generous portion of the chicken mixture followed by a sprinkling of grated Parmesan cheese.

TUE ## Teriyaki Chicken Wraps

These Teriyaki Chicken Wraps make the perfect quick lunch or light supper. Toss everything together, add to a warmed tortilla, roll, and enjoy!

INGREDIENTS

4 flour tortillas

1 pound Perfect Chicken, shredded (see page 6)

1/2 red bell pepper, chopped

1 red onion, chopped

1 (8 ounce) can pineapple pieces, drained

1/2 cup teriyaki sauce

Cilantro for garnish, chopped

Warm the tortillas in a clean, dry skillet for a few minutes per side or in the microwave.

In a mixing bowl, toss together the chicken, bell pepper, onion, pineapple, and teriyaki sauce. Divide the mixture evenly among the tortillas, spooning it down the middle of each one, and garnish with a bit of chopped cilantro. Roll them tightly and serve immediately.

WEEK 4

Spinach Pesto Pasta Bake

For this meal, I wanted something cheesy, pesto-y, and with ground beef. Typically, pesto dishes are made with fish or chicken, but I wanted one with ground beef...so I made one. And it's really good too!

INGREDIENTS

1 pound pasta, any kind

1 pound ground beef

Several tablespoons extra virgin olive oil

1 shallot, chopped

3 to 4 cloves garlic, chopped

1 (10 ounce) package frozen spinach, thawed and drained of excess water

1 (about 7 ounces) jar pesto

1 (3 ounce) package cream cheese, softened

Salt and pepper

1/2 cup reserved cooking liquid (after pasta cooks, reserve about 1/2 cup water from the pot)

1 cup mozzarella cheese, shredded

Parmesan cheese to garnish, grated

Preheat the oven to 425 degrees.

Bring a large pot of water to a boil and drop in the pasta. Cook to al dente (7 or 8 minutes).

Meanwhile, heat a few tablespoons of olive oil over medium-high heat in a large skillet. Add the ground beef and cook until browned and crumbly. Add the shallot and garlic and sauté for 3 to 4 more minutes. Add the spinach, pesto, and cream cheese, and incorporate into the ground beef mixture. Add salt and pepper (as much or as little as you like, probably a few good pinches).

At this time, remove about 1/2 cup water from the pasta pot. Stir the water into the pesto-ground beef mixture. Drain the pasta and add it to the ground beef mixture as well. Pour everything into an 8 x 8-inch baking dish (unless you have an oven-safe skillet), top with mozzarella cheese, and bake until it's brown and bubbly (about 15 minutes).

Remove from the oven and garnish with Parmesan.

Pesto Meatballs

Meatball night is a big deal at my house. The kids love the taste, and I love hiding all sorts of veggies inside. You could prepare this as an appetizer, with pasta, or with a big side salad. My pound of ground beef produced 10 large meatballs, but the size is up to you. You can also use ground turkey instead of beef in this recipe.

INGREDIENTS

1 pound ground beef

3 cloves garlic, chopped

1 cup panko (or other breadcrumbs of your choice)

$\frac{1}{2}$ cup Parmesan cheese, grated

1 box frozen spinach, thawed and excess water squeezed out

$\frac{1}{2}$ cup pesto (store-bought or homemade)

2 eggs, beaten

2 splashes milk

Salt and pepper

1 to 2 tablespoons extra virgin olive oil

Spaghetti sauce for dipping or drizzling on top (optional)

Preheat oven to 425 degrees. In a medium bowl, combine ground beef, garlic, panko, cheese, spinach, pesto, eggs, and milk. Add in just a pinch of salt and pepper. Roll into balls and place on a lightly greased baking sheet (I always line mine with foil for easy cleanup!). Drizzle olive oil over all of the meatballs. Roast in the oven about 20 minutes or until brown.

WEEK 4

Ham and Swiss with Pesto Sandwiches

First, make yummy sandwiches with good stuff...ham and Swiss and pesto. Add a few easy sides...popcorn and strawberries...and you have dinner. (This is a serving for one.)

INGREDIENTS

2 slices bread (or an English muffin or whatever else you like)

Ham, sliced

Swiss cheese, sliced

Pesto

Spinach, cucumbers, bell pepper, other veggies you may like, sliced (optional)

Microwaved popcorn

Strawberries

If you're making this hot, slather both sides of an English muffin with pesto, layer the ham and Swiss, and then place the sandwich under a panini press for about 2 minutes. You could also cook it like a grilled cheese sandwich in a hot skillet.

SAT Bacon and Broccoli Quinoa

This is like a big bowl of comfort food but healthy at the same time. You can serve this as a very hearty side or as a main dish.

INGREDIENTS

2 cups quinoa

3 cups water

8 pieces bacon (I use turkey bacon), chopped

1 shallot, chopped

Extra virgin olive oil

Salt and pepper

3 tablespoons flour

2 cups milk

1½ cups Cheddar cheese, shredded

2 cups broccoli florets

½ cup grated Parmesan cheese

Before you begin, rinse the quinoa off under cold running water. Add quinoa and water to a pot over medium-high heat on the stove. Cover and bring to a boil. Once boiling, reduce heat to low and continue to simmer covered about 10 to 15 minutes.

While the quinoa simmers, place the bacon pieces in a drizzle of olive oil in a skillet over medium-high heat. Allow bacon pieces to crisp up. After they're crispy, add in the chopped shallot and a pinch of salt and pepper. Sauté the shallot a minute or two. Next, sprinkle in the flour and whisk a minute. Next, whisk in the milk and continue to whisk until sauce begins to thicken up. Once sauce starts to thicken up, whisk in the cheese and continue whisking until incorporated.

Pour cooked quinoa into skillet with bacon cheese sauce. Stir in the quinoa and broccoli florets. Sprinkle in Parmesan cheese.

Remove from heat and serve immediately with extra Parmesan.

WEEK 4

SUN Margarita Chicken Soup

This soup kind of just happened. I was in the kitchen thinking of ways to mix and match tortilla soup when it hit me that a "margarita" version might be fun. Add a little Sprite or 7-Up in place of the tequila and a little lime juice, and you have a variation on a classic. Make this in a slow cooker so that when you come in the door, dinner is ready and waiting.

INGREDIENTS

1 pound chicken breasts (frozen or defrosted)

1 (10 ounce) can Ro-Tel tomatoes

1 (12 ounce) can Sprite or 7-Up (can be diet)

1 (15 ounce) can black beans, rinsed and drained

1 (14 ounce) can diced tomatoes

1 (14 ounce) can creamed corn

1 (1 ounce) packet taco seasoning (or 2 tablespoons chili powder)

2 limes, quartered

1 avocado, pit removed and cut into chunks

6 to 8 green onions, chopped (optional)

Cheddar for garnish, shredded (optional)

Layer the first 7 ingredients in a slow cooker. Cover and cook on low for 6 to 8 hours or on high for 3 to 4 hours.

When you're ready to eat, remove the lid and shred the chicken inside the slow cooker with two forks. Ladle the soup into individual bowls and squeeze two quartered limes into each bowl. Garnish with avocado, green onions, and/or Cheddar.

Strawberry Shortcake Trifle

SWEET TREAT

This dessert should be made in advance. I make mine the day before and then wait 24 hours to serve. It's one of my favorites because it's easy, easy, easy and yummy, yummy, yummy. Trust me, your friends and family will love you for making this!

INGREDIENTS

1 (5 ounce) package instant vanilla pudding

3 cups milk

1 (14 ounce) can sweetened condensed milk

1 (12 ounce) container Cool Whip, thawed

1 pound cake, cubed

1 pint fresh strawberries, sliced

In a mixing bowl, combine pudding and milk with a whisk. Then whisk in sweetened condensed milk and Cool Whip. In your serving dish, layer some pound cake pieces, a few strawberry slices, and some of the pudding mixture. Repeat until you reach the top. Keep refrigerated until ready to serve. (The longer it sits in the refrigerator, the better it gets.)

I have layered this dessert in mason jars, trifle dishes, and big bowls. Sometimes I make individual trifles, and sometimes I make one big dessert in a trifle dish. It's up to you!

WEEK 4

Spring Notes

Summer

Week 1 Meal Plan

MON	Chicken Chili Verde
TUE	Greek Tacos
WED	Greek Pasta Salad
THU	Chipotle and Corn Chicken Waffles
FRI	Spinach and Sundried Tomato Joes
SAT	Mango Chicken Tostadas
SUN	Tomatillo and Pineapple Burgers
SWEET TREAT	Hawaiian Luau Bundt Cake

Shopping List

PRODUCE

1 green bell pepper
2 red bell peppers
2 onions
2 red onions
15 to 16 green onions
2 jalapeño peppers
2 limes
1 small cucumber
1 English cucumber
3 pints cherry tomatoes
8 to 10 tomatillos
2 lemons
Fresh oregano (garnish)
Fresh spinach leaves
$\frac{1}{2}$ cup corn kernels (fresh or frozen)
1 to 2 oranges (optional)
2 cups mango chunks (fresh or frozen)
2 avocados
7 to 8 garlic cloves

MEATS

4 to 5 pounds boneless, skinless
   chicken breasts
2 pounds ground turkey
1$\frac{1}{2}$ pounds ground beef

CANNED FOODS,
CONDIMENTS, SOUPS, SAUCES

1 (4 ounce) can chopped green chilies
1 (8 ounce) jar sundried tomatoes in oil
1 (16 to 24 ounce) jar salsa verde
1 (7 ounce) can chipotles in adobo sauce
1 cup chicken stock (can also use water)
Guacamole (enough for a side or garnish)
6 tablespoons hummus
2 (2 ounce) cans sliced black olives
1 (at least 15 ounce) bottle BBQ sauce

2 tablespoons steak seasoning
1 (8 ounce) can pineapple tidbits or crushed
   pineapple
1 (15 ounce) can crushed pineapple
4 cups pineapple juice
1 cup orange juice

GRAINS, PASTA, BREAD

8 corn tortillas
6 taco shells
Tostada shells
1 pound pasta (I use whole wheat penne)
Burger buns (enough for two meals)

FROZEN

2 (10 ounce) packages frozen spinach

BAKING

1 (8.5 ounce) box cornbread muffin mix (with
   ingredients to prepare, per package)
1 (15.25 ounce) box coconut cake mix
2 (3.4 ounce) boxes instant coconut pudding
   (use vanilla if you can't find coconut)
1 (16 ounce) container cream cheese frosting
2 cups sweetened flaked coconut (plus extra
   for garnish)
Maraschino cherries (garnish)

DAIRY

Shredded Monterey Jack or Cheddar cheese
   (garnish)
1 cup fresh feta cheese, crumbled
   (plus extra for garnish)
$\frac{1}{2}$ cup shredded Monterey Jack cheese
4 slices Pepper Jack cheese
4 eggs

MON Chicken Chili Verde

I love this meal because it cooks all day in the slow cooker and then comes together in no time. My kiddos love this because they're into tortillas, chicken, salsa, and guacamole (Texas kids for sure!).

INGREDIENTS

1 pound boneless, skinless chicken breasts

1 green bell pepper, chopped

1 small onion, chopped

1 jalapeño pepper, seeded and chopped

2 (4 ounce) cans chopped green chilies

1 (1 ounce) package taco seasoning (about 2 tablespoons) or 2 tablespoons chili powder

1 (16 to 24 ounce) jar salsa verde

1 cup chicken stock or water

8 tortillas

Guacamole as a side or to garnish

Shredded Monterey Jack or Cheddar cheese to garnish

Squeeze of fresh lime juice, optional

Combine chicken, bell pepper, onion, jalapeño pepper, cans of green chilies, taco seasoning, salsa, and stock or water in slow cooker. Cover and cook on low 6 to 8 hours or on high 3 to 4 hours.

When ready to serve, remove the lid of the slow cooker and shred up the chicken right inside the slow cooker using two forks. Top each tortilla with a little bit of the chicken mixture, some fresh guacamole, a little cheese, and a squeeze of lime juice.

TUE
Greek Tacos

Grab some turkey, a little hummus, fresh veggies, and feta and make your own Greek tacos tonight.

INGREDIENTS

6 taco shells

1 pound ground turkey

1 teaspoon oregano

1 (10 ounce) box frozen spinach, thawed and excess water squeezed out

6 tablespoons hummus, divided

1 red onion, chopped

1 small cucumber, chopped

½ cup cherry tomatoes, halved

Olives, chopped, optional

½ cup fresh feta cheese, crumbled

Extra virgin olive oil

Salt and pepper

Preheat oven to 350 degrees. Place the taco shells on a baking sheet and lightly toast them for about 4 minutes; they burn quickly, so keep an eye on them. Remove from oven and set aside.

Meanwhile, in a large skillet over medium-high heat, drizzle in a tablespoon of olive oil and add the ground turkey. Cook turkey until lightly browned and crumbly, and then add in oregano and spinach. Reduce heat to low and heat a few minutes.

Remove from heat and begin assembling your tacos. Spread 1 tablespoon hummus across the bottom of each shell. Next, add turkey and spinach mixture. Top each taco with onion, cucumber, tomatoes, and olives. Garnish each taco with a little fresh feta.

WED Greek Pasta Salad

This recipe has loads of my favorite Greek flavors all in one easy pasta salad. What I love most about pasta salads is that the longer they hang out in the fridge, the better they get. Have this for dinner one night, and then lunches are ready to go for the next few days.

INGREDIENTS

1 pound pasta, cooked to al dente and then cooled under cold water, drained, and reserved (I use whole wheat penne)

1 red onion, chopped

1 (2 ounce) can sliced black olives, drained

1 English cucumber (so that you can leave the skin on), chopped

1 pint cherry tomatoes, sliced in half

Zest and juice of one lemon
(you need about 2 tablespoons of each)

Extra virgin olive oil

Salt and pepper

Fresh oregano, chopped

Feta cheese, crumbled

After you've cooked and cooled pasta under cold water, drain it well and place it in a large mixing bowl. Next, add the onion, olives, cucumber, tomatoes, lemon zest, and lemon juice followed by several big drizzles of olive oil and a big pinch of salt and pepper. Toss everything together. (Add more olive oil if you feel it needs a touch more.) Next, add as much fresh oregano and feta as you like and toss that together. Cover and refrigerate at least four hours before serving. Toss it one more time before serving.

THU ## Chipotle and Corn Chicken Waffles

This isn't just a meal. It's a feast! For an easy side dish, I like to roast cherry tomatoes in the oven at 425 degrees with a drizzle of olive oil and salt and pepper. Roast about 15 minutes.

INGREDIENTS

4 boneless, skinless chicken breasts

1 (7 ounce) can chipotles in adobo sauce

1 cup orange juice

1 (15 ounce) bottle BBQ sauce

1 box cornbread muffin mix (with ingredients to prepare, per package)

1 red bell pepper, chopped

5 to 6 green onions, chopped

½ cup Monterey Jack cheese, shredded

½ cup corn kernels (frozen or fresh)

A few handfuls fresh spinach leaves

1 pint cherry tomatoes (optional)

Orange slices (optional)

Marinate the chicken with 3 to 4 chipotles, a few spoonfuls of the adobo sauce, the orange juice, and 1 cup BBQ sauce for 30 minutes up to 24 hours. Refrigerate while marinating.

When you're ready to start grilling, remove the chicken breasts from marinade and discard the marinade. Grill the chicken over medium-high heat for about 7 minutes on each side or until the juices run clear and the chicken is fully cooked.

While the chicken is grilling, heat up a waffle iron. Spray with nonstick cooking spray.

In a small bowl, prepare the cornbread mix per package directions for basic cornbread muffins. Into the batter, stir the chopped bell pepper, green onions, cheese, and corn kernels (you can stir them in frozen). Pour the batter into the waffle iron and cook until golden.

Once the chicken is off the grill, add a few spinach leaves to the top of each cooked waffle and then top each waffle with sliced grilled chicken. Finish by drizzling a bit more BBQ sauce over the top.

Serve with roasted cherry tomatoes and/or orange slices (optional).

FRI # Spinach and Sundried Tomato Joes

I took two of my favorite things—turkey meatballs and sloppy joes—and combined them into one. Such a simple, flavorful, and delicious supper.

INGREDIENTS

1 pound ground turkey

4 cloves garlic, minced

1 (10 ounce) package frozen spinach, thawed and drained of excess water

1 (8 ounce) jar sundried tomatoes in oil, drained

2 teaspoons lemon zest

Feta cheese, crumbled to garnish

Green onions, chopped, to garnish

Salt and pepper

Extra virgin olive oil

Burger buns

In a large skillet over medium-high heat, brown turkey in a drizzle of olive oil until browned and crumbly. Add in a liberal pinch of salt and pepper. Stir in garlic, spinach, sundried tomatoes, and lemon zest. Reduce heat to medium and let simmer about 5 minutes or until everything is heated through.

Take each burger bun and top with a generous portion of ground turkey mixture. Garnish with feta cheese and chopped green onions.

SAT ## Mango Chicken Tostadas

To change up tostadas at our house, we add a bunch of veggies and some nice mango instead of using our normal Tex-Mex flavors. By the way, frozen mangoes in a bag are divine if fresh mangoes are not available. And the coconut lovers in our house added toasted coconut. (Put your coconut in a dry skillet and brown just slightly over medium-low heat.)

INGREDIENTS

1 pound boneless, skinless chicken breasts, uncooked

4 cups pineapple juice (plus a little water to cover)

2 cups mango chunks (fresh or frozen)

1 red bell pepper, chopped and seeded

1 avocado, chopped into chunks

8 green onions, chopped

Salt and pepper

Tostada shells

Toasted coconut to garnish (optional)

In a slow cooker, layer the chicken and add the pineapple juice. (If you still need to cover the chicken with more liquid, add water until the chicken is covered.) Cover and cook on low for 6 to 8 hours or on high for 3 hours. The last 30 minutes your supper is cooking, shred the chicken right inside the slow cooker with two forks, turn the heat to high, and add the mango and chopped bell pepper. Cover and cook the remaining 30 minutes.

Using a slotted spoon, remove the chicken, mango, and pepper and put it all into a bowl (discard the liquid). Add bits of avocado and chopped green onion. Sprinkle with salt and pepper. Top each tostada shell with the chicken mixture. If you're using toasted coconut, sprinkle it on top now.

Tomatillo and Pineapple Burgers

Burgers are a summertime necessity—but they don't have to be boring burgers! I've used home-made salsa in this recipe, but if you want to go the simple route, go ahead and use store-bought tomatillo salsa. Either way, you're going to love the flavor combination! The sweetness of the pineapple really pairs well with the spiciness of the jalapeño pepper and cheese.

INGREDIENTS

1½ pounds ground beef

2 tablespoons steak seasoning

8 to 10 tomatillos, husks removed and rinsed off

3 to 4 garlic cloves

1 onion, sliced

1 jalapeño pepper, sliced (remove seeds for a less spicy version)

Juice of one lime

1 (8 ounce) can pineapple tidbits or crushed pineapple, drained

1 avocado, sliced

4 slices Pepper Jack cheese

Salt and pepper

Burger buns

To make the salsa, combine tomatillos, garlic, onion, jalapeño pepper, and lime juice in the bowl of your food processor. Pulse until it reaches desired consistency. Stir in pineapple. Refrigerate until ready to eat. (For a simpler version, stir pineapple into store-bought tomatillo salsa.)

Preheat outdoor grill or indoor grill pan to medium-high. In a mixing bowl, combine ground beef with steak seasoning and a little salt and pepper. Divide ground beef mixture into 4 burger patties. Grill about 6 minutes each side. Add a slice of cheese on top about a minute before they're done.

To assemble your burgers, take one bun and top with burger patty, sliced avocado, and tomatillo-pineapple salsa. Serve open faced.

SWEET TREAT  *Hawaiian Luau Bundt Cake*

Even if you can't go to the islands, you can eat a cake that brings the island flavors to you. Aloha.

INGREDIENTS

1 box coconut cake mix

2 small boxes instant coconut pudding (or vanilla if you can't find it)

$\frac{1}{2}$ cup vegetable oil

1 (15 ounce) can crushed pineapple (reserve the juice!), divided

1 cup canned pineapple juice

$\frac{1}{4}$ cup water (or more pineapple juice if your can has any left)

4 eggs

1 container cream cheese frosting

2 cups sweetened, flaked coconut, divided

Maraschino cherries to garnish (optional)

Preheat oven to 350 degrees and grease a 10-inch Bundt pan. In mixing bowl, combine cake mix, puddings, oil, pineapple juice, water, and eggs with electric mixer. Stir in 1 cup crushed pineapple and one cup coconut. Pour into prepared pan and bake 40 to 45 minutes, or until toothpick inserted comes out clean. Let cake rest on counter in pan 10 minutes. Invert cake onto serving plate to finish cooling.

Stir remaining cup coconut into store-bought frosting and frost cooled cake. Top cake with cherries.

Week 2 Meal Plan

MON	Tex-Mex Ravioli Bake
TUE	Grilled Shrimp Tacos
WED	Spicy Shrimp Pasta
THU	Pineapple Teriyaki Salmon
FRI	Buffalo Chicken Paninis
SAT	Grilled Chicken with Blackberry Salsa
SUN	Ranch Burgers with Avocado Ranch Sauce
SWEET TREAT	Key Lime Pie Bars

Shopping List

PRODUCE

10 to 12 green onions
3 red onions
1 onion
1 (8 to 12 ounce) package cabbage/slaw mix
1 avocado
1 lime
2 to 4 key limes
1 red bell pepper
2 cups fresh spinach
2 pints blackberries
1 jalapeño
1 large tomato
1 bunch cilantro
2 cups spinach leaves

MEATS

2 pounds peeled and deveined shrimp
4 (6 ounce) salmon fillets
4 chicken breasts
1 pound grilled chicken
1 pound ground beef

CANNED FOODS, CONDIMENTS, SOUPS, SAUCES

1 (10 ounce) can Ro-Tel tomatoes
1 (8 ounce) can tomato sauce
1 (15 ounce) can black beans
1 cup ranch dressing
1 (1 ounce) packet ranch dressing seasoning mix
1 cup chicken stock
1 (6 ounce) can pineapple juice
$\frac{1}{4}$ cup soy sauce
$\frac{1}{8}$ cup red wine vinegar
$\frac{1}{4}$ teaspoon garlic powder
Lemon pepper seasoning
$\frac{1}{2}$ cup sesame seeds
$\frac{1}{2}$ cup buffalo sauce

GRAINS, PASTA, BREAD

2 (9 ounce) packages cheese ravioli
1 pound angel hair pasta
Crushed tortilla chips or tortilla strips (garnish)
Tortillas
1 loaf bakery bread, sliced
Burger buns (enough to feed your family)

FROZEN

1 cup frozen corn

BAKING

1 (15.25 ounce) box yellow cake mix

DAIRY

1 cup shredded Cheddar cheese
1 (4 ounce) container bleu cheese crumbles
1 (8 ounce) package cream cheese
4 eggs

MON **Tex-Mex Ravioli Bake**

Easy cleanup is important when you're cooking with kids! We like to make this recipe when my husband is out of town. We use cheese ravioli, which makes the meal vegetarian, but you could most definitely use beef or chicken ravioli instead. The bottom line is...this supper is so simple! Simple to make and simple to clean up. Score one for mom!

INGREDIENTS

2 (9 ounce) packages cheese ravioli

10 to 12 green onions, chopped

1 (10 ounce) can Ro-Tel tomatoes

1 (15 ounce) can black beans, drained and rinsed

1 (8 ounce) can tomato sauce

1 cup frozen corn

1 tablespoon chili powder (or a 1 ounce packet taco seasoning)

1 cup Cheddar cheese, shredded

Preheat the oven to 425 degrees.

Grease (I use Pam) a pie plate or an 8 x 8-inch baking dish. Set it aside.

Bring a large pot of water to a boil over medium-high heat. Add the ravioli and cook it until al dente (about 4 minutes). Drain the water and reserve the ravioli.

Meanwhile, in a mixing bowl, combine the green onions (reserve a few for garnish), Ro-Tel tomatoes, black beans, tomato sauce, corn, and chili powder.

Pour the cooked ravioli across the bottom of your prepared baking dish and then top it with the black bean mixture. Sprinkle cheese on top of everything and bake it for 15 to 20 minutes or until the casserole is nice and bubbly and the cheese has melted.

Remove from the oven and serve.

TUE *Grilled Shrimp Tacos*

There is just something about summer and shrimp tacos. They go together perfectly... especially when enjoyed on a patio.

INGREDIENTS

1 pound peeled and deveined shrimp

2 tablespoons chili powder

1 package cabbage/slaw mix (found by the prepackaged salads)

1 avocado, sliced

1 red onion, diced

1 lime, quartered

Ranch dressing

Tortilla chips or tortilla strips, crushed

Tortillas

Preheat outdoor grill or indoor grill pan to medium high. In a bowl, combine shrimp and chili powder. Skewer your shrimp or put them in a fish/shrimp basket before placing them on your hot grill. Grill each side about a minute or two or until nice and charred.

Remove shrimp from grill and assemble tacos. We put down our tortillas first and then top it with a little slaw, some sliced avocado, a little red onion, a few shrimp, a squirt of lime juice, a drizzle of Ranch, and a few pieces of tortilla chips for crunch.

WED Spicy Shrimp Pasta

I love shrimp. It's so versatile, easy to work with, and quick cooking. All things I am looking for when making supper for my family. This dish comes together in minutes. I make ours spicy, but you can tame it to suit your family's tastes.

INGREDIENTS

1 pound angel hair pasta

1 onion, chopped

1 red bell pepper, chopped

Extra virgin olive oil

Salt and pepper

1 pound cooked and deveined frozen shrimp, thawed per package directions

1½ teaspoons red pepper flakes (use less for mild)

1 cup chicken stock

2 cups fresh spinach

Drop your pasta in a pot of boiling water and cook to al dente (about 5 minutes). Meanwhile, in a big skillet over medium-high heat, sauté the chopped onion and bell pepper in a drizzle of olive oil with a pinch of salt and pepper. Cook about 5 minutes.

Next, add in the shrimp and red pepper flakes and cook about a minute. Pour in the chicken stock and deglaze the pan (scrape the little bits off the bottom). Reduce heat to low.

Drain pasta and add to skillet. Stir to incorporate pasta with the other ingredients. Stir in fresh spinach and let it wilt about a minute.

So fast, right? The angel hair pasta cooks up in minutes and the shrimp is already cooked, so all you're doing is heating it through.

THU
Pineapple Teriyaki Salmon

We eat quite a bit of fish during the spring and summer months. Grilled salmon is one of our favorite go-tos. You can toss the fish on the grill or bake it in the oven. Either way you do it, you will love the flavor!

INGREDIENTS

4 (6 ounce) salmon fillets

$\frac{1}{4}$ cup soy sauce

1 (6 ounce) can pineapple juice

$\frac{1}{8}$ cup red wine vinegar

3 tablespoons sugar

$\frac{1}{4}$ teaspoon garlic powder

$\frac{1}{2}$ cup sesame seeds

Place the salmon fillets in a large baggie along with all of the ingredients above (except sesame seeds). Put the baggie in the fridge and marinate as long as you can (at least 1 hour and up to 24 hours), turning the bag periodically to make sure the salmon is well coated. Discard the marinade before grilling or baking.

If baking, preheat the oven to 400 degrees. Line a baking sheet with foil and lightly spray with Pam. Place each piece of salmon on the baking sheet and bake about 6 minutes per side. Remove from the oven and serve with toasted sesame seeds.

If grilling, preheat a grill to medium-high heat. (We place each piece of fish in a fish basket on top of our grill so the fish doesn't flake off through the grates.) Grill each side of the fish about 4 minutes. Remove from the grill and serve with toasted sesame seeds.

Note: To toast sesame seeds, add them to a clean, dry skillet and toast over medium-high heat about a minute. Remove from the heat and reserve for garnishing.

FRI ## *Buffalo Chicken Paninis*

I love grilling chicken breasts for dinner one night and using the leftovers the next night in a completely different way. This summer, you should totally be grilling extra chicken each time you're out there. This sandwich makes for the perfect quick weeknight meal, post-swim supper, or dinner when you just flat-out don't want to cook. I use rye bread, but you can try sourdough, wheat, multigrain, French bread...whatever you have, it works.

INGREDIENTS

1 loaf bakery bread, sliced

1 pound grilled chicken, cut into bite-sized
   pieces or strips

1/2 cup of your favorite buffalo hot sauce

2 cups spinach leaves

Bleu cheese crumbles

Preheat panini press or large skillet. Lightly grease with cooking spray. In a bowl, toss grilled chicken with buffalo sauce; set aside.

Take two slices of bread; top one slice with chicken, spinach, and a sprinkle of bleu cheese and then top with the second slice of bread. Place sandwich under the panini press for about 5 minutes or until golden and the cheese is melted. Slice in half and serve with your favorite chips.

If you don't have a panini press, just place each panini in a skillet over medium-high heat and set another skillet on top of your sandwich (to press it down). After about 4 minutes, flip your sandwich and press the other side down.

SAT Grilled Chicken with Blackberry Salsa

Confession: I don't like grilled chicken. Does that make me weird? But my kids and hubby love grilled chicken...sigh...so if it's on the menu, I have to jazz it up. This quick and flavorful blackberry salsa turns grilled chicken into a meal I like. We dip chips in it too—it's that good. Easy and delicious!

INGREDIENTS

Extra virgin olive oil

4 chicken breasts

Salt and pepper

Lemon pepper seasoning

1 red onion, chopped

2 pints blackberries

1 jalapeño, chopped
  (remove the seeds and ribs for less heat)

1 large tomato, chopped

A handful of cilantro, chopped

Preheat an outdoor grill or indoor grill pan to medium-high heat.

Drizzle some olive oil on top of the chicken breasts, followed by a good pinch of salt, pepper, and lemon pepper seasoning. Rub the seasonings on the chicken and then place on the grill. Grill 8 minutes or so on each side.

While the chicken is grilling, make the salsa. In a mixing bowl, combine the red onion, blackberries, jalapeño, tomato, and cilantro. Take a fork and lightly mash the ingredients together just a bit. (You don't want to break up the salsa too much.) Cover and refrigerate until you're ready to serve.

Once the chicken is grilled to perfection, plate and top with the salsa.

SUN ## Ranch Burgers with Avocado Ranch Sauce

Ranch burgers are pretty common, but add a little avocado ranch sauce and they're out of this world. Easy. Simple. Done.

INGREDIENTS

1 pound ground beef

1 (1 ounce) packet ranch dressing seasoning mix

1 avocado

1 cup bottled ranch dressing

Red onion slices

Burger buns

Preheat your outdoor grill or indoor grill pan to medium-high. In a mixing bowl, combine ground beef with ranch seasoning mix. Divide ground beef mixture into 4 burger patties. Grill about 6 minutes each side.

While the burgers are on the grill, place sliced avocado pieces in a food processor. Add in ranch dressing and pulse until combined. (If you don't have a food processor, just use your hand mixer.) Remove burgers from the grill. Top bun with burger patty, avocado ranch sauce, and sliced onion.

SWEET TREAT

Key Lime Pie Bars

If you can't find key limes at your grocery store, use a regular lime instead. You'll need about 4 key limes or 2 regular limes for this recipe.

INGREDIENTS

1 box yellow cake mix

4 eggs

½ cup butter, melted

1 box powdered sugar (about 4 cups)

1 (8 ounce) package cream cheese, softened

2 tablespoons key lime zest

4 tablespoons fresh key lime juice

Preheat the oven to 350 degrees and grease a 9 x 13-inch baking dish. In a large mixing bowl, combine cake mix, 2 eggs, and melted butter. Spread in bottom of pan. In a second bowl, beat powdered sugar, 2 more eggs, cream cheese, lime zest, and lime juice until smooth. Spread cream cheese mixture on top of crust mixture.

Bake 35 to 40 minutes until edges are brown and center is set (it will still be slightly wobbly in the middle). Cool on counter 30 minutes, then refrigerate 2 hours or up to 2 days.

Week 3 Meal Plan

MON	Chicken Fajita Tacos
TUE	Grilled Shrimp and Pineapple Tacos
WED	BLT Pasta
THU	Enchiladas Suizas
FRI	Honey Mustard Chicken and Corn Wraps
SAT	Grilled Shrimp and Bacon Salad
SUN	Bleu Cheese Baked Steaks
SWEET TREAT	Watermelon Cupcakes

Shopping List

PRODUCE

3 red onions

8 to 11 green onions

1 jalapeño

1 green bell pepper

1 fresh pineapple

3 avocados

1 head purple cabbage

2 limes

1 head garlic

2 pints cherry tomatoes

4 cups spinach leaves

8 to 10 basil leaves

8 cups romaine lettuce

3 cups corn kernels (fresh or frozen)

$1\frac{1}{4}$ cups pureed watermelon

MEATS

Fajita chicken (enough to feed your family)

2 pounds peeled and deveined shrimp (can be fresh or frozen)

18 to 20 slices bacon

2 pounds chicken

4 filet mignon steaks (or whatever cut you prefer)

CANNED FOODS, CONDIMENTS, SOUPS, SAUCES

Aioli (garnish)

$1\frac{1}{2}$ cups chicken broth

1 (10.5 ounce) can cream of mushroom soup

1 (4 ounce) can chopped green chilies

1 (15 ounce) can tomatillo or green chili enchilada sauce

1 (16 ounce) bottle honey mustard salad dressing (I use Newman's Own)

Montreal steak seasoning

GRAINS, PASTA, BREAD

8 corn tortillas (or 16 small, street-style tortillas)

8 tortillas (your favorite type for enchiladas)

4 large tortillas (flour, corn, or whole wheat)

1 pound pasta (I use whole wheat penne)

BAKING

1 (15.25 ounce) box white cake mix

Pink food coloring (optional)

2 cups powdered sugar

DAIRY

$\frac{1}{2}$ cup grated Parmesan cheese

1 cup shredded Swiss cheese (plus extra for garnish)

$\frac{1}{2}$ cup shredded Pepper Jack cheese

1 cup bleu cheese crumbles

4 eggs

MON Chicken Fajita Tacos

During the summer, who wants to be inside fussing with food when you can be outside swimming, biking, golfing, and hanging out with family and friends? You can either buy preseasoned, uncooked fajita chicken or season your own with a little taco seasoning or chili powder. Then throw the ingredients on a baking tray, pop it in the oven, and forget about it until you're ready to eat. Don't forget the guacamole!

INGREDIENTS

Fajita chicken (we use a chicken that was uncooked but already seasoned for fajitas from our butcher's counter)

1 red onion, chopped

1 jalapeño, seeds removed and sliced

1 green bell pepper, sliced

Extra virgin olive oil

Salt and pepper (I love a good kosher salt)

Preheat the oven to 400 degrees. Line a baking sheet with foil and then spray with Pam (for easy cleanup).

Line up the meat and veggies on your baking sheet (try not to overcrowd). Drizzle a liberal amount of olive oil over everything (several big tablespoons) and then sprinkle on a generous pinch of salt and pepper. Place the tray in the oven and roast for 30 to 35 minutes. When you pull out the tray, the veggies will be tender and the chicken cooked to perfection. Serve with corn tortillas, salsa, sour cream, and guacamole.

Grilled Shrimp and Pineapple Tacos

We grilled some shrimp. We grilled some pineapple. We made a little avocado mash. Added a touch of aioli. Put everything on tortillas. Dinner was done!

INGREDIENTS

1 pound cooked and deveined shrimp (fresh or frozen that has been thawed)

2 tablespoons chili powder

Salt and pepper

1 fresh pineapple, cut into 4 or 5 large pieces (the bigger pieces make it easier to grill)

2 avocados, chopped into small pieces

Kosher or sea salt

Store-bought aioli

1 purple cabbage, shredded

1 red onion, chopped

Zest and juice of two limes

8 corn tortillas (we use 16 of the small, street taco–style tortillas)

Preheat an indoor grill pan or outdoor grill to medium-high.

Place the shrimp in a large bowl. Make sure they are somewhat dry. (I blot them with a paper towel if they're too wet.) Sprinkle with chili powder along with a pinch of salt and pepper. Toss until the shrimp are well coated with the seasonings.

If your grates are too large for shrimp (they'll fall through), then use a grilling basket. Spray your grate or your grilling basket quite liberally with cooking spray so the shrimp won't stick.

Add the shrimp to the grill and grill a few minutes (about 3 minutes per side). At the same time, lay the pineapple pieces across the grill and grill them 3 or 4 minutes too (flipping them over halfway). Remove the shrimp and pineapple from the grill.

Using a fork, mash the avocado pieces with a pinch of sea salt. Also, cut the grilled pineapple pieces into smaller chunks. Then assemble your tacos: tortillas, cabbage, avocado mash, shrimp, pineapple, aioli, chopped red onion, and a little lime zest followed by a squeeze of fresh lime juice.

  *BLT Pasta*

The roasted garlic is the star of this dish. Roasting your garlic makes the cloves tender and sweet while giving your dish a caramelized flavor that is delicious. A simple step gives a huge boost of flavor.

INGREDIENTS

1 bulb garlic

Extra virgin olive oil

Salt and pepper

1 pint cherry tomatoes

1 pound pasta (we use whole wheat penne)

10 to 12 slices bacon, chopped

1½ cups chicken broth

2 cups spinach leaves (just grab the kind next to the bagged salads)

½ cup Parmesan cheese, grated

8 to 10 basil leaves, torn or chopped

Preheat oven to 450 degrees. Take an entire bulb of garlic and chop off the top. Drizzle olive oil over the exposed cloves and sprinkle with salt and pepper. Wrap the bulb in foil and place on a baking sheet. Roast in the oven for 30 minutes.

On another baking sheet, spread out cherry tomatoes. Drizzle with oil and sprinkle with salt and pepper. After the garlic has been in the oven 30 minutes, move it onto the tomato baking sheet. Cook an additional 15 minutes.

While the tomatoes and garlic are roasting, bring a pot of water to boil. Cook pasta until al dente.

Over medium-high heat, add a couple tablespoons of olive oil to a skillet. Once hot, add chopped bacon to brown (about 6 minutes). Add chicken broth and lots of salt and pepper to the pan and then deglaze the pan (scrape up the little bits from the bottom). Lower the heat to medium-low and simmer 3 to 5 minutes. Unwrap the garlic from the foil and remove the roasted cloves with a fork (they will be tender). Stir in spinach, roasted tomatoes, and roasted garlic pieces. Drain pasta and add to bacon mixture. Stir in cheese and basil.

THU *Enchilada Suizas*

Swiss cheese. In an enchilada. Love. I used to think enchiladas were too much hassle for a weeknight, but if you use my Perfect Chicken method they'll come together in no time!

INGREDIENTS

1 pound Perfect Chicken (see page 6)

1 can cream of mushroom soup

1 (4 ounce) can chopped green chilies

Salt and pepper

1 cup Swiss cheese, shredded (plus a little extra for garnish)

½ cup Pepper Jack cheese, shredded

8 tortillas

1 (15 ounce) can tomatillo or green chili enchilada sauce

Chopped green onions to garnish

Preheat oven to 400 degrees and lightly grease an 8 x 8-inch baking dish with cooking spray. Set aside.

In a large mixing bowl, combine the shredded chicken with cream of mushroom soup, green chilies, a liberal pinch of salt and pepper, and both cheeses. Once combined, spread a little of the mixture down the center of each tortilla. Roll and place seam side down in the prepared baking dish. Once all 8 enchiladas are tucked inside the dish, pour enchilada sauce over top.

Bake uncovered about 20 minutes, or until the edges are slightly browned and everything is bubbling. Remove from oven and garnish with chopped green onion and extra Swiss cheese.

Honey Mustard Chicken and Corn Wraps

I made these little wraps one day for lunch and then thought, *These would make a great dinner too!* Simple enough for lunch but hearty and yummy enough to serve for dinner.

INGREDIENTS

1 pound Perfect Chicken, shredded (see page 6)

1 cup or so of your favorite honey mustard salad dressing

1 cup corn kernels, frozen or fresh, at room temperature

6 to 8 green onions, chopped

About 2 cups of fresh spinach leaves

Pinch of salt and pepper

4 large tortillas (flour, corn, or whole wheat)

In a mixing bowl, combine the chicken with the honey mustard dressing, corn, and green onions. Add salt and pepper to taste.

Lay out the four tortillas and place a few spinach leaves down the center of each one. Spoon the chicken mixture over the spinach. Wrap up the tortillas, and you're ready for lunch.

So simple! I wrapped up my tortilla in a paper towel and then placed it in a baggie and headed off to the pool. The perfect little lunch and a great way to use up leftover chicken.

SAT Grilled Shrimp and Bacon Salad

Oh, goodness. How we love to grill shrimp. The key to grilling shrimp is either putting it on a skewer, using a grilling basket or a cedar plank, or even using an aluminum cookie sheet. You just don't want your shrimp falling through the grill grates. A big batch of grilled shrimp...some crunchy bacon...your favorite salad toppings... It's super tasty and super simple.

INGREDIENTS

1 pound uncooked shrimp, peeled and deveined
  (ask your fishmonger at the grocery store)

2 tablespoons chili powder

8 cups romaine lettuce
  (a big handful for each person)

8 pieces cooked bacon, crumbled
  (we use turkey bacon)

1 avocado, diced

1 pint cherry tomatoes, halved

1 red onion, diced

2 cups corn kernels (fresh or frozen that you've
  heated up a bit)

Bleu cheese for garnish, crumbled

A drizzle of honey mustard salad dressing
  (we use Newman's Own)

Preheat an outdoor grill or indoor grill pan to medium-high heat.

Toss the shrimp with the chili powder and then grill just a few minutes on each side.

Arrange plates with lettuce, bacon, avocado, tomatoes, onion, and corn. Top with a few pieces of grilled shrimp and bleu cheese crumbles. Drizzle the salad dressing on top.

SUN *Bleu Cheese Baked Steaks*

My husband makes us these steaks a lot, and they are so good! I know everyone has their own particular way of preparing a steak, but for what it's worth, this is our favorite method.

INGREDIENTS

4 filet mignons (you can use whatever cut you prefer)

Worcestershire sauce

Montreal steak seasoning

1 tablespoon butter per steak, softened

1 tablespoon bleu cheese crumbles per steak

Preheat an outdoor grill or indoor grill pan to as hot as it will go. (Our grill goes to 600 degrees, so that's the temperature we use. Get it HOT!) Also, preheat the oven to 450 degrees. Prepare a 9 x 13-inch baking dish by spraying it with cooking spray.

Pour 1 or 2 tablespoons of Worcestershire sauce and 1 tablespoon of steak seasoning over the top of each steak and rub the sauce and seasoning on both sides.

Place the steaks on the hot grill, searing for about 2 minutes each side. (You're not cooking them on the grill. You're just searing them for color and to lock moisture in.) After 2 minutes, remove them from the grill, place them in the baking dish, and put them in the oven to bake. Bake them 15 minutes for a steak cooked medium and longer for more well done.

While the steaks are baking, make a bleu cheese butter by combining a tablespoon of butter with a tablespoon of bleu cheese. (They're both soft, so they should mix up well with just a spoon.)

When the steaks are cooked to your preference, remove them from the oven and put the bleu cheese butter on top of each steak. Pop the steaks back in the oven for 2 to 3 more minutes to allow the butter to melt a bit. Remove from the oven and serve.

SWEET TREAT ## Watermelon Cupcakes

I puree fresh watermelon in my blender but you can also buy frozen watermelon in the freezer department (it comes in a liquid form ready for smoothies) and defrost that. No matter how you get your watermelon, you are going to love these delicious cupcakes.

INGREDIENTS

1 box white cake mix

1¼ cups pureed watermelon, divided

½ cup vegetable oil

4 egg whites

Pink food coloring, optional

½ cup butter, softened

2 cups powdered sugar

Preheat oven to 350 degrees. Line 2 (12 count) muffin tins with paper liners. Set aside.

In a large mixing bowl, beat white cake mix, 1 cup pureed watermelon, vegetable oil, and egg whites with an electric mixer. Beat in a drop or two of pink food coloring.

Pour batter into prepared muffin tins and bake 19 to 21 minutes or until a toothpick inserted in the middle comes out clean. Allow cupcakes to cool in tin about 10 minutes before removing them to wire racks to finish cooling.

Meanwhile, in a mixing bowl, beat the butter, remaining ¼ cup pureed watermelon, and powdered sugar until blended. Add more watermelon if the frosting is too thick or more sugar if it's too thin. Beat in a drop or two of pink food coloring.

Frost cooled cupcakes with Watermelon Frosting. Store in the refrigerator when not enjoying.

Week 4 Meal Plan

MON	Summer Corn Chowder
TUE	Pineapple-Lime Chicken Tostadas
WED	Cucumber and Dill Pasta Salad
THU	Crab Cakes with Honey Dijon Dressing
FRI	Brisket Ranch Sandwiches
SAT	Grilled Cod with Avocado Pea Mash
SUN	Caesar Salad Burgers
SWEET TREAT	Red, White, and Blue Trifle

Shopping List

PRODUCE

5 red onions

4 jalapeños

4 red potatoes

3 cups corn kernels (fresh or frozen)

2 cups peas (fresh or frozen)

10 to 14 chives

2 limes

1 lemon

6 avocados

1 clove garlic

1 tomato

Cilantro (garnish)

1 English cucumber

4 tablespoons chopped dill

Field greens (optional)

1 head romaine lettuce

2 cups sliced fresh strawberries

1 cup blueberries

MEATS

1 pound kielbasa-style sausages
   (I use turkey sausage)

6 slices bacon (I use turkey bacon)

1 pound chicken

12 ounces lump crabmeat

4 pieces cod

2 pounds brisket (flat and trimmed)

2 pounds ground turkey

2 chopped anchovy fillets (optional)

CANNED FOODS, CONDIMENTS, SOUPS, SAUCES

2 (10 ounce) cans Ro-Tel tomatoes

1 quart chicken stock

4 cups beef stock

1 (20 ounce) can crushed pineapple

3 tablespoons Old Bay seasoning

4 tablespoons Dijon mustard

1 (4 ounce) bottle liquid smoke (use either
   hickory or mesquite flavored)

½ tablespoon apple cider vinegar

1 tablespoon honey

Caesar salad dressing (for drizzling)

2 cups ranch dressing

Guacamole (enough for a side)

GRAINS, PASTA, BREAD

Tostada shells

1 pound elbow pasta

1 cup plain breadcrumbs

4 to 6 hoagie rolls

4 pieces Texas toast

FROZEN

1 (10 ounce) package frozen spinach

BAKING

1 box (5 ounce) instant vanilla pudding

1 angel food cake

1 (14 ounce) can sweetened condensed milk

DAIRY

Half-and-half or milk

Crème fraîche (garnish)

2 eggs

1 cup grated Parmesan cheese
   (plus extra for garnish)

1 (12 ounce) container Cool Whip

1 (8 ounce) container sour cream

MON Summer Corn Chowder

During the summer, I sometimes like a corn chowder...but because it's 100 degrees in my house, I don't want it thick and creamy. This recipe whips up in no time and is a great way to use up fresh corn (but you can substitute frozen corn just fine). To top things off? A dollop of crème fraîche... because that stuff is good stirred into *anything*. (You can use sour cream in a pinch.)

INGREDIENTS

Extra virgin olive oil

1 pound kielbasa-style sausage, cut into pieces (we use turkey sausage)

1 red onion, chopped

6 slices bacon, chopped (we use turkey bacon)

Salt and pepper

1 jalapeño, chopped (for less heat, remove the seeds and ribs)

1 (10 ounce) can Ro-Tel tomatoes

4 red potatoes, quartered

1 quart chicken stock

3 cups fresh or frozen corn kernels

Splash of cream or milk

Crème fraîche for garnish

Chives for garnish, snipped

In a large pot over medium-high heat, add in a big drizzle of olive oil along with the sausage, onion, and bacon. Sprinkle a big pinch of salt and pepper over that mixture. Allow the onion to caramelize and the bacon to crisp up (5 to 8 minutes). When the onion is tender and the bacon is crisp, stir in the jalapeño and sauté a minute or two. Next, stir in the tomatoes, potatoes, and stock. (You need enough stock to cover everything.) Stir in another pinch of salt and pepper, bring everything to a boil, and then reduce the heat to low and simmer until the potatoes are tender (about 10 minutes). Then stir in the corn and let the chowder cook another 3 to 4 minutes.

Just before you're ready to serve, stir in a splash (a tablespoon or two) of cream or milk. Ladle the chowder into bowls and garnish with a dollop of crème fraîche (or sour cream) and chives.

TUE Pineapple-Lime Chicken Tostadas

Pineapple and lime are a match made in heaven! Add them to Perfect Chicken with some gua-camole, chopped jalapeño, and cilantro, and you have a restaurant-style dinner on the table in minutes. Your family will never believe this all started in the slow cooker.

INGREDIENTS

1 pound Perfect Chicken, shredded (see page 6)

1 (20 ounce) can crushed pineapple

Zest and juice of one lime (about 2 tablespoons of each), reserving a little zest for serving

1 jalapeño, chopped (seed it if you would like less heat)

1 (10 ounce) can Ro-Tel tomatoes, drained

Tostada shells

Guacamole

Cilantro for garnish, chopped

In a mixing bowl, stir together the chicken, crushed pineapple, lime zest (remember to save a bit for later!), lime juice, jalapeño, and tomatoes.

Assemble your tostadas in this order: start with the shell and then add a generous portion of guacamole, some of the pineapple chicken mixture, and top with cilantro. Add just a touch of lime zest to the top to finish things off.

Cucumber and Dill Pasta Salad

Oh, goodness. I love me some dill. Dill and cubed cucumber...such a good combination! Perfect for a simple summer supper.

INGREDIENTS

1 pound elbow pasta, cooked to al dente, drained and cooled off with cold water

1 red onion, chopped

1 English cucumber, chopped

4 tablespoons dill, chopped

1 cup ranch dressing

Salt and pepper

In a large mixing bowl, combine all of the ingredients. Cover and chill at least 3 hours (and up to 24) before serving. Garnish with a little more dill when serving.

Note: After you cook the pasta, make sure you drain it and then run cold water over the top to cool it down before draining it again really well. Also, I use an English cucumber so I don't have to peel it, but you can substitute it with two regular cucumbers, peeled.

THU

Crab Cakes with Honey Dijon Dressing

We love crab cakes at our house. If you've never made them before, you should! It's kind of like making a meatball—you just mix up the ingredients and bake.

INGREDIENTS

12 ounces lump crabmeat

2 teaspoons Old Bay seasoning

1 cup plain breadcrumbs

2 eggs, lightly beaten

8 to 12 chives, chopped (reserve some for garnish)

4 tablespoons Dijon mustard, divided

Zest of one lemon (about 2 tablespoons total)

½ tablespoon apple cider vinegar

1 tablespoon honey

1 cup extra virgin olive oil

Salt and pepper

Field greens (optional)

Strawberries, sliced (optional)

Preheat the oven to 400 degrees. Line a cookie sheet with foil or parchment paper and lightly spray with Pam. Set aside.

In a large mixing bowl, combine the crabmeat, Old Bay seasoning, breadcrumbs, eggs, chives, 1 tablespoon of mustard, and lemon zest. Take the mixture and turn it into 12 small crab cake patties with your hands. Place the patties on the prepared cookie sheet. Bake 10 to 12 minutes or until lightly browned.

Meanwhile, prepare the honey mustard dressing. In a bowl, whisk together the remaining three tablespoons of mustard with the apple cider vinegar and honey. Whisk in the olive oil. (If the dressing is too thick, whisk in a bit more olive oil. If it's too thin, add a touch more mustard and/or honey.) Once the dressing reaches the desired consistency, whisk in a pinch of salt and pepper.

When the crab cakes are done baking, remove from the oven and assemble on a plate. Add some field greens and sliced strawberries and spoon the honey Dijon dressing over everything.

FRI Brisket Ranch Sandwiches

On a hot August day, it's nice not to heat up the kitchen with the stove and oven. Instead, I let my slow cooker do all the work!

INGREDIENTS

2 pounds brisket (flat and trimmed)

1 (4 ounce) bottle liquid smoke
(use either hickory or mesquite flavored)

4 cups beef stock

Extra virgin olive oil

Salt and pepper

A few handfuls of romaine lettuce

2 avocados, sliced

Ranch salad dressing

1 red onion, chopped

4 to 6 hoagie rolls, split in half

In a large pot over medium-high heat, brown both sides of the brisket in about two tablespoons of olive oil. Salt and pepper each side of the brisket quite liberally. After each side is browned (about 3 minutes per side) add brisket to slow cooker along with the entire bottle of liquid smoke and beef stock. Cover and cook on low about 8 hours or on high 4 hours.

When you're ready to assemble your sandwiches, remove brisket from slow cooker (discard all liquid) and slice it up on your cutting board. Take each dinner roll and top with romaine lettuce, sliced brisket, several pieces of avocado, chopped red onion, and a drizzle of ranch.

SAT Grilled Cod with Avocado Pea Mash

One of my favorite meals in England is fish and chips with a side of mushy peas (basically, they're smashed green peas). I married that yummy idea with a little Tex-Mex. The result? Devoured! And my guacamole-loving children didn't even notice the peas inside.

INGREDIENTS

4 pieces cod

1 tablespoon Old Bay seasoning

Salt and pepper (we love kosher or sea salt)

2 cups peas, divided (fresh or frozen but have been thawed)

2 avocados, pits removed and scooped out

1 jalapeño, chopped (remove the ribs and seeds for less heat)

1 to 2 tablespoons fresh lime juice

1 red onion, chopped

Preheat outdoor grill or indoor grill pan to medium-high heat.

Take each of the four pieces of cod and sprinkle with Old Bay seasoning (just a little bit on each one, front and back). Next, add a nice pinch of salt and pepper to each fillet. Grill the cod for 4 minutes or so on each side (they'll grill up quickly!).

Meanwhile, make the avocado mash. Place 1 cup of the peas along with the avocados, jalapeños, lime juice, and a pinch of salt in a bowl. Using two forks or a potato masher, mash up this mixture until it's the texture of guacamole. Once it has reached the desired consistency, stir in the remaining cup of peas. (Check to see if you need to add more salt.)

To serve, plate the grilled cod with a big dollop of avocado pea mash right on top followed by chopped red onion.

WEEK 4

 Caesar Salad Burgers

It's a turkey burger that tastes like a chicken Caesar salad. You pile your Caesar salad toppings on top and put everything on a big piece of Texas toast like a giant crouton.

INGREDIENTS

2 pounds ground turkey

3 tablespoons extra virgin olive oil

2 anchovy fillets, chopped (optional)

1 cup grated Parmesan cheese, plus a little more for garnishing

1 (10 ounce) package frozen spinach, defrosted and all of the excess liquid squeezed out

Romaine lettuce leaves torn for topping

Drizzles of your favorite Caesar salad dressing

4 pieces Texas toast, toasted

Preheat your outdoor grill or indoor grill pan to medium-high heat.

Add the olive oil, chopped anchovy fillets (optional), one cup Parmesan, and spinach to ground turkey. Divide turkey into four sections and make four patties. Grill patties about 8 minutes per side or until cooked through.

Add your cooked burger patty to a piece of Texas toast and then top with romaine lettuce and drizzles of your favorite Caesar dressing. Garnish with a little more Parmesan.

Red, White, and Blue Trifle

Every year on the Fourth of July, we have some sort of strawberry and blueberry dessert because it looks all fun and patriotic. This year, I took angel food cake from my grocery store's bakery and turned our annual treat into a trifle. Burgers, swimming, fireworks, watermelon, and this dessert are all you need on your Fourth.

INGREDIENTS

1 (5 ounce) box instant vanilla pudding

1 can sweetened condensed milk

$\frac{1}{2}$ cup water

1 (12 ounce) container Cool Whip, thawed

1 (8 ounce) container sour cream

1 angel food cake, cut into big pieces

About 2 cups fresh strawberries, sliced

About one cup blueberries

In a large bowl, combine pudding, milk, and water with a whisk. Refrigerate this mixture 5 minutes. Remove from fridge and stir in Cool Whip and sour cream until smooth.

In a large trifle dish (or individual dishes), layer angel food cake across the bottom, add a layer of strawberry slices and a few blueberries over the cake, then add $\frac{1}{3}$ of your pudding mixture. Repeat 3 times. Finish off with a few more strawberries and blueberries on top to garnish.

Refrigerate at least 4 hours and up to 2 days before serving.

WEEK 4

Summer Notes

Fall

Week 1 Meal Plan

MON	Sweet Potato Shepherd's Pie
TUE	Mexican Lettuce Wraps
WED	Butternut Squash Mac and Cheese
THU	Chicken à la King
FRI	BBQ Apple Chicken Sandwiches
SAT	Roasted Chicken and Sweet Potato Risotto
SUN	Enchilada Chili
SWEET TREAT	Pumpkin Spice Cupcakes

Shopping List

PRODUCE

4 onions

3 shallots (or red onions)

1 red onion

4 to 5 green onions

2 sweet potatoes plus a few more
(enough for 2 cups mashed)

8 large lettuce leaves

2 avocados

1 clove garlic

1 jalapeño

1 tomato

4 tablespoons chopped fresh thyme

MEATS

2 pounds ground beef

2½ pounds boneless, skinless chicken breasts

1 rotisserie chicken

1 pound ground beef, turkey, or chicken

CANNED FOODS, CONDIMENTS, SOUPS, SAUCES

2 (10 ounce) cans cream of mushroom soup

1 (15 ounce) can chili beans

1 (10 ounce) can Ro-Tel tomatoes

1 (14 ounce) can Ro-Tel tomatoes

1 (10 ounce) can enchilada sauce

1 (15 ounce) can mild chili beans

1 (15 ounce) can pumpkin puree

1 (16 ounce) bottle BBQ sauce

2 quarts chicken stock

2 cups apple juice or cider

Guacamole (enough for a side or garnish)

GRAINS, PASTA, BREAD

1 pound short-cut pasta (I use shells)

1 cup Arborio rice

Tortilla chips (garnish)

Large biscuits or toast (enough to feed
your family)

Toast, burger buns, or rolls (enough to feed
your family)

FROZEN

1 (10 ounce) package frozen peas and carrots

1 (10 ounce) package butternut squash, thawed
and pureed

2 cups frozen peas

2½ cups frozen corn

BAKING

1 tablespoon cinnamon or pumpkin pie spice

1 cup pumpkin spice chips

4 cups powdered sugar

DAIRY

Shredded Pepper Jack cheese (garnish)

1 cup milk plus 1 tablespoon milk

1 cup shredded Cheddar cheese

1 cup grated Parmesan cheese (plus extra
for garnish)

Shredded cheese (garnish, for chili)

Sour cream (garnish)

4 eggs

1 (8 ounce) package cream cheese

MON ## Sweet Potato Shepherd's Pie

Have no fear if sweet potatoes aren't your thing: You can totally substitute a basic mashed potato instead! This is a super simple weeknight meal—meat and potatoes all in one place.

INGREDIENTS

1 pound ground beef

1 onion, chopped

1 (10 ounce) can cream of mushroom soup

1 (10 ounce) package frozen peas and carrots

2 cups mashed sweet potatoes

Extra virgin olive oil

Salt and pepper

Preheat oven to 400 degrees. In a large skillet over medium-high heat, brown ground beef in a drizzle of olive oil until crumbly; drain fat. Stir in onion and sauté a few minutes. Add in a generous pinch of salt and pepper. Reduce heat to low and stir in cream of mushroom soup and frozen veggies. When combined, pour mixture into a greased 8 x 8-inch baking dish. Spread mashed potatoes all over the top, covering the meat completely.

Pop casserole into the oven and bake about 15 minutes, or until everything is bubbly. Remove from oven and serve.

TUE Mexican Lettuce Wraps

I'm calling these Mexican Lettuce Wraps, but, really, they're like tacos without the tortilla shell. The filling simmers away all day in your slow cooker, and then you wrap, top, and roll come dinner time.

INGREDIENTS

1 pound ground beef

Extra virgin olive oil

Salt and pepper

2 tablespoons chili powder

1 (15 ounce) can chili beans

1 (10 ounce) can Ro-Tel tomatoes

About 8 large lettuce leaves

Guacamole for garnish

Pepper Jack cheese for garnish, shredded

Green onion for garnish, chopped

In a skillet over medium-high heat, brown ground beef in a drizzle of olive oil. Once browned and crumbly, stir in a big pinch of both salt and pepper and the chili powder. Pour this mixture into your slow cooker, and then add the chili beans and tomatoes. Cover and cook on low for 6 to 8 hours or on high for 3 to 4 hours. When you're ready to serve, take a lettuce leaf and add a big dollop of meat to each one followed by your favorite garnishes.

WED Butternut Squash Mac and Cheese

I'm always looking for ways to add butternut squash or pumpkin to our family's fall dishes. I love the flavor, and I also love the extra boost of veggies—with all those good vitamins—for my kiddos. The other night, we made this for dinner along with some brisket, and it was a huge hit!

INGREDIENTS

1 pound short-cut pasta (I use shells)

Extra virgin olive oil

1 shallot (or red onion), diced

2 tablespoons flour

1 cup milk

1 cup Cheddar cheese, shredded

1 (10 ounce) package butternut squash, thawed and pureed

¼ cup Parmesan cheese, grated (plus a little extra for garnish)

About 4 tablespoons fresh thyme, roughly chopped

Salt and pepper

Bring a large pot of water to a boil over medium-high heat and add the pasta. Cook until al dente (about 6 or 7 minutes).

Meanwhile, in a large saucepan over medium-high heat, sauté the shallot in about 2 tablespoons of olive oil and a nice pinch of salt and pepper for about 3 minutes or until nice and tender. Add another drizzle of olive oil. Next, whisk in the flour and cook about 1 minute. Then whisk in the milk. Whisk everything together about a minute before whisking in the pureed squash. Continue whisking over medium-high heat until the sauce thickens (it takes a couple of minutes). Once the sauce is thick enough to coat your spoon, whisk in the Cheddar and Parmesan cheese along with the thyme.

Drain the water from the cooked pasta and pour the squash mixture on top of the pasta. Serve immediately and garnish with a little extra Parmesan and thyme.

THU

Chicken à la King

You can be totally versatile on your carb choices. I like a traditional biscuit with mine, but you can use toast, cornbread, or an English muffin—or be like my hubby and go without! This meal is simple and happy—perfect for family suppers.

INGREDIENTS

1½ pound boneless, skinless chicken breasts, frozen or thawed

½ onion, chopped

1 can cream of chicken soup

2 tablespoons flour

1 cup frozen peas

1 cup frozen corn

Salt and pepper

Biscuits or toast for serving

Layer the first 4 ingredients in your slow cooker. Give it a quick stir and then cover and cook on low 6 to 7 hours or on high 3 to 4 hours.

About 30 minutes before serving, take two forks and shred the chicken right inside your slow cooker. Next, stir in frozen peas and corn with a generous pinch of salt and pepper. Cover and cook on high another 20 to 30 minutes. Spoon chicken mixture over the top of the biscuits and serve.

BBQ Apple Chicken Sandwiches

FRI

I just adore a slow-cooker meal that is super simple and waiting when I'm ready to eat. Apples, onions, and slow cookers are staples at our house in the fall! The apple juice adds sweetness to this dish without being overpowering, and the chicken cooks up juicy and tender.

INGREDIENTS

1 pound boneless, skinless chicken breasts, frozen or thawed

2 cups apple juice or cider

1 (16 ounce) bottle BBQ sauce

1 onion, sliced and sautéed (optional)

Toast, burger buns, or rolls to serve

In your slow cooker, combine chicken, apple juice or cider, and entire bottle of BBQ sauce. Cook on low 6 to 8 hours or on high 3 to 4 hours. When dinner is ready, remove chicken and some sauce from slow cooker into a bowl. Shred chicken with two forks (add in a little more sauce if needed). Serve shredded chicken with sautéed onions (optional) on top of your favorite bread.

SAT

Roasted Chicken and Sweet Potato Risotto

This meal is super easy when you buy a rotisserie chicken from the grocery store. And though it looks fancy, it can be on your dinner table in 30 minutes. Relax. Risotto is a cinch.

INGREDIENTS

2 quarts chicken stock

Extra virgin olive oil

2 shallots or 1 red onion, chopped

1 cup Arborio rice

1 rotisserie chicken, meat removed from the bones and set aside

2 sweet potatoes, cooked and the insides scooped out and roughly chopped up

1 cup frozen peas

½ cup Parmesan cheese, grated

Salt and pepper

In a large stockpot, bring the chicken stock to a low simmer. (Not boiling, just a simmer. Put a lid on the pot to trap the liquid inside.)

In a separate pan, heat 2 tablespoons of olive oil over medium-high heat. Add the shallots or onion and cook 4 to 5 minutes. Stir in the rice for another minute.

Take a ladle and add 1 cup of the hot stock to the rice. Stir constantly for a minute or so. As the liquid evaporates, the rice will become super starchy and delicious. Stir often, adding stock every time the majority of the liquid evaporates. Continue doing this for 18 to 20 minutes. Add stock, stir, wait for it to evaporate, and add more. This will cause the risotto to fluff up and look creamy (without using any cream!). A lot of recipes will tell you to stir continuously, but you don't need to. Just stir it well every few minutes, and you'll be fine.

After the rice is tender (take a bite!), stir in the rotisserie chicken, sweet potatoes, and peas. Continue cooking another 5 to 6 minutes. (It doesn't take long for everything to heat up in the risotto.) Stir in the cheese and season with salt and pepper to taste.

SUN Enchilada Chili

This chili is great because it's a one-pound meal (meaning you can use ground beef, ground turkey or ground chicken), it's a one-pot meal (you won't have other dirty dishes to clean up), it comes together in minutes, and it's really delicious!

INGREDIENTS

1 pound ground beef, turkey, or chicken

Extra virgin olive oil

Salt and pepper

1 tablespoon chili powder

1 onion, chopped

1 (14 ounce) can Ro-Tel tomatoes

1 (10 ounce) can enchilada sauce

1½ cups frozen corn

1 (15 ounce) can mild chili beans, undrained

Tortilla chips, shredded cheese, chopped green onion, sour cream to garnish

In a large pot over medium-high heat, brown ground meat in a drizzle of olive oil with a pinch of salt and pepper. Once brown, stir in chili powder and chopped onion and sauté a few minutes. Stir in tomatoes, enchilada sauce, corn, and beans. Reduce heat to low and cook about 10 minutes. Ladle chili into bowls and garnish with your favorite toppings.

SWEET TREAT *Pumpkin Spice Cupcakes*

A little pumpkin, a little spice, a lot of yummy!

INGREDIENTS

2 cups sugar

1½ cups vegetable oil

4 eggs

2 cups flour

1 teaspoon salt

2 teaspoons baking soda

1 tablespoon cinnamon or pumpkin pie spice

1 (15 ounce) can pumpkin purée

1 cup pumpkin spice chips, optional

1 (8 ounce) package cream cheese, softened

½ cup butter, softened

1 teaspoon vanilla

4 cups powdered sugar

1 tablespoon milk

Preheat oven to 350 degrees. Line 3 (12 count) muffin tins with cupcake liners or spray one 9 x 13-inch baking dish with cooking spray; set aside.

In a mixing bowl combine sugar, vegetable oil, and eggs with an electric mixer; set aside. In a separate mixing bowl, combine flour, salt, baking soda, and cinnamon with a fork or whisk. Slowly beat the flour mixture into the sugar mixture. Mix until just combined. Next, beat in pumpkin until just combined. Stir in your pumpkin chips (optional).

Pour batter into prepared baking dish or divide between your muffin tins. Bake cupcakes 14 to 16 minutes, or until a toothpick inserted in the middle comes out clean. If you're using a 9 x 13-inch baking dish, bake about 40 minutes. Allow to cool completely before frosting.

To make the frosting, beat the cream cheese, butter, vanilla, powdered sugar, and milk together. Add more milk if the frosting is too thick and more powdered sugar if it's too thin. Frost cooled cupcakes and store in fridge if not serving immediately.

Week 2 Meal Plan

MON	Sausage and Broccoli Tortellini Bake
TUE	Crunchy BBQ Brisket Tacos
WED	Sausage and Butternut Squash Pasta
THU	Brown Sugar Brisket
FRI	Maple Mustard Chicken Sandwiches
SAT	Mom's Jambalaya
SUN	Sausage and Pumpkin Soup
SWEET TREAT	Caramel Apple Bread Pudding

Shopping List

PRODUCE

4 onions

8 cloves garlic

14 to 16 green onions

3 onions

2 cups chopped broccolini

Basil (garnish)

Parsley (garnish)

1 cup grated apples (Granny Smith; you can also use 1 cup applesauce)

MEATS

3 pounds Italian sausage

1 (2 to 3 pounds) brisket

1 (3 to 5 pounds) flat-trimmed brisket

2 pounds boneless, skinless chicken breasts

8 ounces sausage links

2 handfuls frozen shrimp (peeled and deveined)

CANNED FOODS, CONDIMENTS, SOUPS, SAUCES

4 cups chicken stock

2 cups salsa

3 to 4 cups BBQ sauce

1 tablespoon fennel seed (optional)

4 cups apple juice (or 2 cups apple juice and 2 cups water)

1 (15 ounce) can pumpkin (I use Libby's)

1 (14 ounce) can diced tomatoes

1 (14 ounce) can Ro-Tel tomatoes

2 (10 ounce) cans chicken broth

1 tablespoon Cajun seasoning

3 tablespoons maple syrup

GRAINS, PASTA, BREAD

2 (9 ounce) packages cheese-filled tortellini or ravioli

Crunchy taco shells

1 pound pasta

1½ cups uncooked long grain rice

Burger buns (enough to feed your family)

1 loaf challah or brioche

FROZEN

1 (12 ounce) box frozen butternut squash

BAKING

1 cup breadcrumbs

1 cup brown sugar

1 tablespoon cinnamon

1 cup pecan pieces

1 (12 ounce) jar caramel topping

DAIRY

2 tablespoons milk, half-and-half, or cream

6 cups milk plus 2 tablespoons

½ cup grated Parmesan cheese (plus extra for garnish)

Monterey Jack cheese (garnish)

1 cup grated Cheddar cheese

3 eggs

MON Sausage and Broccoli Tortellini Bake

This casserole is fast and simple. I chopped up some broccolini for this version, but you can use broccoli florets, cauliflower, or asparagus. This method is all about assembly: Grab some broccolini, grab some sausage (or even a brat!), grab some refrigerated tortellini (ravioli works too), assemble, bake, and eat.

INGREDIENTS

2 (9 ounce) packages cheese-filled tortellini or ravioli

1 pound Italian sausage

Extra virgin olive oil

3 cloves garlic, chopped

8 to 10 green onions, chopped

1 cup chicken stock

2 cups chopped broccolini

2 tablespoons milk, half-and-half, or cream

1 cup breadcrumbs

1/2 cup Parmesan cheese, grated

Preheat oven to 400 degrees and grease an 8 x 8-inch baking dish. Bring a large pot of water to a boil. Drop in tortellini and cook about 5 minutes. Drain water and set tortellini aside.

Meanwhile, in a large skillet over medium-high heat, cook up sausage in a drizzle of olive oil. Once sausage is brown and crumbly, add garlic, green onions, and chicken stock. Reduce heat to low and let your mixture simmer just a minute or two. Add broccolini and reserved tortellini. Stir in milk. Pour sausage mixture into prepared baking dish. Sprinkle breadcrumbs and Parmesan cheese over the top. Bake about 15 minutes uncovered or until the casserole is bubbling and a little brown around the edges. Remove from oven and serve.

To make in advance, assemble the casserole but don't bake it. At this point, you could cover and refrigerate the casserole or freeze it. You will need to adjust your baking time to about 25 minutes if it's coming from the fridge or 40 minutes if it's coming from the freezer.

TUE Crunchy BBQ Brisket Tacos

You'll come home from a busy day, and your brisket will be all cooked and tender in the slow cooker. All you do is add a little BBQ sauce and a few garnishes and you're done!

INGREDIENTS

Extra virgin olive oil

Salt and pepper

1 (2 to 3 pound) brisket

2 cups salsa

1 to 1½ cups water

1 to 2 cups BBQ sauce

Crunchy taco shells

Chopped green onions and/or Monterey Jack cheese to garnish

Preheat a heavy pot with olive oil over medium-high heat. Salt and pepper the brisket, and brown each side in the pot 4 to 5 minutes. Make sure you salt and pepper each side. Transfer brisket to a slow cooker and pour salsa over the top. Pour a little water over everything until the brisket is mostly covered in the salsa and water. Cover and cook on low 7 to 8 hours or on high 4 to 5 hours.

About 20 minutes before serving, remove brisket to cutting board and cover with foil. This will allow the meat to rest and the juices to redistribute and keep it moist. Discard all of the liquid in the slow cooker.

After your brisket has cooled about 10 minutes, slice and chop it into pieces and place those pieces into a bowl. Once all of your chopped beef is in a bowl, add BBQ sauce and coat everything. Use as much BBQ sauce as you think your family will love.

Take each taco shell (you should get 6 to 8, depending on how much brisket you use) and stuff it with brisket mixture. Finally, garnish tacos with some shredded cheese and chopped onions.

WED Sausage and Butternut Squash Pasta

Check your freezer department for a box of frozen butternut squash. All you do is bring it home and thaw it. If you would rather roast your own squash, see below for directions.

INGREDIENTS

1 pound sausage (pork or chicken)

1 pound pasta

1 onion, chopped

3 cloves garlic, chopped

1 tablespoon fennel seed (optional)

½ cup chicken stock

2 tablespoons flour

2 tablespoons milk

1 (12 ounce) box frozen butternut squash, thawed

1 cup Cheddar cheese, grated

Handful chopped basil, optional

Over medium-high heat, brown sausage until cooked through and crumbly; drain fat. Add in onions and garlic and sauté about 5 minutes. Meanwhile, bring a large pot of water to a boil, drop in pasta, and cook to al dente (about 7 to 8 minutes).

Stir the fennel seed into sausage and add chicken stock to deglaze the pan (scrape all the little bits off the bottom). Simmer over low heat a minute or two.

Whisk flour and milk into sausage for a minute to create a roux. Stir in thawed squash and cheese. Reduce heat to low and let everything simmer together about 5 minutes.

Drain pasta and add to sausage mixture. Stir until covered in sauce. Top with basil (optional).

Note: Roasting your own butternut squash is simple! Preheat oven to 425 degrees. Split a butternut squash down the middle, scrape out the seeds, drizzle a few tablespoons of extra virgin olive oil over the tops, and season with salt and pepper. Roast on a baking sheet about 30 minutes. Remove from oven and scrape out the insides of the squash. Stir about 2 cups into this pasta dinner.

THU Brown Sugar Brisket

This brisket is particularly yummy because it has a brown sugar and mustard glaze over it. I serve this with baked potatoes and a green salad, but mashed potatoes would be yummy too! Or pile this up on a bun and serve it as a sandwich with a side of potato salad or chips. As for the leftovers, add some brisket and Monterey Jack cheese to a tortilla and make a quesadilla or taco. I used apple juice as my cooking liquid because it adds great flavor to the meat, but you can cut the amount of apple juice in half by using water too.

INGREDIENTS

1 (3 to 5 pounds) flat-trimmed brisket

1/2 cup brown sugar

1 tablespoon yellow mustard

1 onion, chopped

4 cups apple juice (or 2 cups apple juice and 2 cups water)

Salt and pepper

Extra virgin olive oil

Season brisket with salt and pepper. Heat olive oil in a large skillet over medium-high heat and brown each side of brisket, about 4 minutes per side. While it's browning, combine the brown sugar and mustard together in a small bowl; set aside.

Place browned brisket in the slow cooker. Rub brown sugar mixture all over the brisket. Add chopped onion and pour apple juice on top. Cover and cook on high about 8 hours.

When you're ready to eat, open the lid and remove the brisket from the liquid (discard the liquid) to a cutting board. Shred the brisket and serve.

FRI Maple Mustard Chicken Sandwiches

Maple shines in this little supper recipe. It's so easy. You put all of the ingredients in a slow cooker, and at the end of the day, dinner is done.

INGREDIENTS

1 pound boneless, skinless chicken breasts

2 cups BBQ sauce (we use Sweet Baby Ray's)

2 tablespoons yellow mustard

3 tablespoons maple syrup (a good quality one!)

$\frac{1}{2}$ cup chicken stock

4 burger buns

Green onions for garnish, chopped

Place the chicken, BBQ sauce, mustard, maple syrup, and stock in a slow cooker. Cover and cook on low for 6 to 8 hours or on high for 3 to 4 hours. When you're ready to eat, remove the lid and shred the chicken inside the slow cooker using two forks. Top burger buns with the shredded chicken mixture followed by some green onions.

SAT Mom's Jambalaya

I'm not Cajun, but I love me some jambalaya! My mama adds chicken, sausage, and shrimp, but you can mix and match. I prefer a nice, smoky pork sausage, but any sausage you use is fine. Note my instructions for cooking the rice for this dish. Bonus tip: You can use a store-bought jambalaya mix instead of your own rice and seasoning and make this dish on top of the stove.

INGREDIENTS

1 pound boneless, skinless chicken breasts, uncooked and cut into pieces

8 ounces sausage links, cut into 1-inch pieces

1 (14 ounce) can diced tomatoes

1 (14 ounce) can Ro-Tel tomatoes

2 (10 ounce) cans chicken broth

1 tablespoon Cajun seasoning

1 teaspoon cumin

1½ cups long grain rice, uncooked

2 handfuls frozen shrimp

In a slow cooker, layer the chicken, sausage, tomatoes, Ro-Tel tomatoes, chicken broth, and both kinds of seasoning. Cook on low for 6 to 8 hours or on high for 3 to 4 hours. If you're using a standard, not fast-cooking long grain rice, then 1 hour before you're ready to eat, add the rice and cover. If you're using a quick-cooking rice, then add about 20 minutes before you're ready to eat. Add the shrimp 10 minutes before you're ready to eat.

SUN Sausage and Pumpkin Soup

Every fall, I like to make savory pumpkin dishes. And this soup is a winner...so much flavor in one little bowl. Bonus? It comes together in no time flat in one pot.

INGREDIENTS

1 pound sweet Italian sausage (remove from casings if necessary)

Extra virgin olive oil

1 onion, chopped

2 cloves garlic, chopped

Salt and pepper

3 tablespoons butter

3 tablespoons flour

2 cups milk (I use 2%)

2 cups chicken stock

1 (15 ounce) can pumpkin (I use Libby's)

Parmesan cheese for garnish, grated

Parsley for garnish, chopped

In a large pot over medium-high heat, brown the sausage in just a drizzle of olive oil. Once it's browned and crumbly, stir in the onion and garlic along with a big pinch of salt and pepper and sauté about five minutes (until tender). Next, stir in the butter and allow it to melt. As soon as it does, sprinkle in the flour and stir about a minute. Next, whisk in the milk, chicken stock, and pumpkin. Bring everything to a boil, reduce the heat to low, and simmer 10 minutes. Ladle the soup into bowls and garnish with grated Parmesan and chopped parsley.

 SWEET TREAT

Caramel Apple Bread Pudding

If you've never made bread pudding before, this is your chance. It's warm and cozy and perfect for chilly nights. I made this bread pudding for dinner guests and then served it in mason jars instead of bowls or plates. Serve alone, with a dollop of whipped cream, or with a scoop of ice cream—you can't go wrong!

INGREDIENTS

1 loaf challah or brioche, torn into pieces

4 cups milk

3 eggs, lightly beaten

1 cup grated apples (I use 2 Granny Smiths and grate them with my cheese grater, or substitute 1 cup applesauce)

1 cup sugar

1 cup brown sugar

1 tablespoon cinnamon

1 cup pecan pieces

1 (12 ounce) jar caramel topping, divided

Preheat oven to 350 degrees and grease a 9 x 13-inch baking dish. Tear bread into bite-sized pieces and place them in baking dish. Pour milk over bread and let stand about 10 minutes.

Stir eggs together with the grated apple, sugar, brown sugar, cinnamon, pecan pieces, and ½ cup caramel topping. Pour this mixture over bread mixture. Bake uncovered for 40 to 45 minutes.

Remove from oven and serve immediately. I cut mine into portions and then drizzle additional caramel topping over each piece. If you're serving this in a mason jar or trifle dish, drizzle caramel in between layers of bread pudding.

Week 3 Meal Plan

MON	Pumpkin and Sausage Potpie
TUE	Sesame Chicken Tostadas
WED	Chipotle Pumpkin Pasta
THU	Cider Chicken and Roasted Sweet Potatoes
FRI	Old-Fashioned Sloppy Joes
SAT	Pizza Meatballs
SUN	Chicken Noodle Soup
SWEET TREAT	Pumpkin Spice Latte Cake

Shopping List

PRODUCE

5 onions
10 to 11 cloves garlic
10 to 12 green onions
2 large sweet potatoes
2 apples (I use Granny Smith)
Parsley (garnish)
Cilantro (garnish)

MEATS

2 pounds ground Italian sausage (I use sweet
  pork sausage)
1 pound chicken
4 chicken breast halves
1 pound boneless, skinless chicken breasts
2 pounds ground beef
$\frac{1}{2}$ cup pepperoni

CANNED FOODS, CONDIMENTS, SOUPS, SAUCES

$\frac{1}{2}$ cup soy sauce
$\frac{1}{4}$ cup sesame seeds
2 (14 ounce) cans diced tomatoes
2 (8 ounce) cans tomato sauce
1 (6 ounce) can tomato paste
1 can chipotles in adobo sauce
3 (15 ounce) cans pumpkin (I use Libby's)
$3\frac{1}{2}$ cups chicken stock
Garlic powder
$1\frac{1}{2}$ cups apple cider
1 (14 ounce) jar pizza sauce
1 (10 ounce) can cream of chicken soup
1 (14 ounce) can creamed corn

GRAINS, PASTA, BREAD

1 (16 ounce) can biscuits (I use Grand's)
4 tostada shells
1 pound small pasta (I use elbow noodles)
1 pound rigatoni pasta
Burger buns (enough to feed your family)

FROZEN

3 (10 ounce) packages frozen vegetable medley
  (carrots and peas work well)

BAKING

3 tablespoons brown sugar
1 (15.25 ounce) box spice cake mix
2 (3.4 ounce) boxes instant vanilla pudding
4 cups powdered sugar
2 tablespoons cinnamon

DAIRY

Grated Parmesan cheese (garnish)
$\frac{1}{2}$ cup shredded mozzarella cheese
6 eggs
Milk (3 to 4 splashes)

MON Pumpkin and Sausage Potpie

I love to whip up potpies in the fall, and I also love to make savory pumpkin dishes. I combined the two ideas, and this yummy supper was born. It's hearty, savory, flavorful, and family friendly. So quick and simple for busy fall nights.

INGREDIENTS

1 pound ground Italian sausage (I use a sweet pork sausage)

Extra virgin olive oil

1 onion, chopped

3 cloves garlic, chopped

Salt and pepper

1 (15 ounce) can pumpkin (I use Libby's)

2 cups frozen peas and carrots mix

1 (16 ounce) can biscuits (I use Grand's)

Preheat the oven to 375 degrees. Grease either an 8 x 8-inch baking dish or four individual oven-safe bowls (I use Pam). Set aside.

In a large skillet over medium-high heat, sauté the sausage in olive oil. Once it's browned and crumbly, add the onion, garlic, and a pinch of salt and pepper. Sauté just a few minutes or until the onion is tender. Stir in the pumpkin and frozen veggies and heat through (3 to 4 minutes).

Pour the ground beef mixture into the prepared baking dish and then top with the uncooked biscuits. If you're using individual serving dishes, top each bowl with two biscuits.

Place serving dish(es) in the oven and bake 10 minutes or until the tops of biscuits are browned. Removed from oven and serve immediately.

Now, the bottoms of your biscuits won't brown because they're resting on the potpie mixture. We love them this way, but if you want your entire biscuit cooked through, you'll need to bake them separately (perhaps while the mixture is simmering on the stove), and then just top potpie mixture with the biscuits and immediately serve. Either way, delish!

TUE Sesame Chicken Tostadas

Tonight's dinner is a unique spin on the tostada...instead of Mexican inspired, it's Asian inspired. So fun, right? Feel free to mix and match your ingredients.

INGREDIENTS

1 tablespoon sesame oil or extra virgin olive oil

2 garlic cloves, chopped

1 pound cooked and shredded chicken

½ cup soy sauce

¼ cup toasted sesame seeds

8 to 10 green onions, chopped

4 tostada shells

In a large skillet over medium-high heat, drizzle either sesame oil or olive oil. Add the garlic and sauté a minute. Next, add the chicken and soy sauce and heat through for just a few minutes. (The chicken is already cooked, so you're just heating it up with the garlic and soy sauce.)

Spoon the chicken mixture onto the tostada shells and garnish with a few toasted sesame seeds and chopped green onions.

Note: I toast my sesame seeds in a dry skillet over medium heat for about 2 minutes. So simple and full of flavor!

WED Chipotle Pumpkin Pasta

The bright orange goodness of pumpkin pairs perfectly with so many dishes. You can kick up this recipe a notch by adding chipotle peppers. Two peppers give a good amount of heat. One is better for kiddos who don't like very much heat, and three are great for those who like it hot (like me!).

INGREDIENTS

1 pound rigatoni pasta

1 pound Italian-style chicken sausages, cut into rounds (or use beef or pork)

Extra virgin olive oil

1 onion, chopped

3 cloves garlic, chopped

Salt and pepper

1 (14 ounce) can diced tomatoes

1 (8 ounce) can tomato sauce

1 (15 ounce) can pumpkin (I use Libby's)

1 can chipotles in adobo sauce, divided

Parmesan cheese for garnish, grated

Bring a large pot of water to a boil. Add the pasta and cook it until al dente (6 to 7 minutes). Drain and reserve.

In a large skillet over medium-high heat, brown the sausage rounds in 3 tablespoons of olive oil. Once they're browned on both sides, add the onion and garlic, followed by a big pinch of salt and pepper. Continue until the onions are tender. Next, stir in tomatoes, tomato sauce, and pumpkin.

Open the can of chipotles and remove as many as you would like. Chop them and add to the sauce along with a tablespoon or so of the sauce from the can. (You can freeze or refrigerate the remaining peppers in the can.) Reduce the heat to low and allow everything to simmer together for 5 minutes. Add the cooked pasta to the sauce and stir. Dish the pasta into bowls and garnish with Parmesan cheese.

THU ## Cider Chicken and Roasted Sweet Potatoes

Winner, winner...I have a chicken dinner! If you love chicken, sweet potatoes, and apple cider, this recipe is perfect. The chicken cooks on the stove while the sweet potatoes crisp up in the oven.

INGREDIENTS

2 large sweet potatoes, diced into cubes

Extra virgin olive oil

Coarse black pepper

Sea salt or kosher salt

4 chicken breast halves

Garlic powder

1 large onion, chopped

2 apples, chopped (we use Granny Smith)

$1\frac{1}{2}$ cups apple cider

$1\frac{1}{2}$ cups chicken stock

Parsley or cilantro for garnish, chopped

Preheat the oven to 425 degrees. Cover a baking sheet with foil and spray with Pam.

Spread the sweet potatoes on the prepared baking sheet. Drizzle a liberal amount of olive oil (about ¼ cup) over the tops of the potatoes, followed by a few generous pinches of salt and pepper. Toss the potatoes so they're equally covered in olive oil and seasoning. Roast in the oven 15 minutes. Toss them, then roast another 15 minutes.

In a large skillet over medium-high heat, add a few tablespoons of olive oil. Sprinkle salt, pepper, and garlic powder on both sides of each chicken breast. Get the skillet nice and hot, and then carefully place seasoned chicken on it. Brown the chicken on one side (about 5 minutes), and then brown the second side. Next, add the onion and apples to the skillet and sprinkle with salt and pepper. When the chicken is browned on both sides and the onion is starting to get tender, pour in the cider and stock. Bring this mixture to a boil, and then turn the heat to low and simmer for 20 minutes.

When you're ready to serve, remove the potatoes from the oven and serve hot alongside a piece of chicken and some onion and apples.

FRI Old-Fashioned Sloppy Joes

You just can't beat an old-fashioned sloppy joe. My version simmers all day in the slow cooker and then is ready and waiting come suppertime.

INGREDIENTS

1 pound ground beef
Extra virgin olive oil
Large pinch of both salt and pepper
1 (6 ounce) can tomato paste
1 (8 ounce) can tomato sauce
1 (14 ounce) can diced tomatoes

3 tablespoons Worcestershire sauce
1 tablespoon mustard
3 tablespoons brown sugar
4 burger buns
Green onions for garnish, chopped

In a large skillet over medium-high heat, brown the ground beef in a drizzle of olive oil. Once browned and crumbly, add in a liberal pinch of both salt and pepper before transferring the meat to your slow cooker. Next, add the tomato paste, tomato sauce, tomatoes, Worcestershire sauce, mustard, and brown sugar. Stir and then cover with the lid and cook on low for 6 to 8 hours or on high for 3 hours. When you're ready to serve, add a generous scoop of sloppy joe mixture to the burger buns and garnish with green onions.

SAT Pizza Meatballs

My kids love pizza and they love meatballs, so I made some meatballs that taste like pizza! My hubby and I eat our meatballs with a side salad, but my kiddos have theirs over buttered noodles. No matter how you serve them, they'll eat them.

INGREDIENTS

1 pound ground beef

1 onion, chopped

2 to 3 cloves garlic, chopped

2 tablespoons Italian seasoning

1/2 cup mozzarella cheese, shredded

2 eggs

1/2 cup pepperoni, chopped

1 (14 ounce) jar pizza sauce

Parmesan cheese, grated to garnish

Preheat oven to 425 degrees. Line a baking sheet with foil and spray with cooking spray; set aside. In a large mixing bowl, combine ground beef, onion, garlic, Italian seasoning, cheese, eggs, and pepperoni. Shape the meat mixture into 12 golf-ball-sized meatballs. Place meatballs on prepared pan and roast 15 to 18 minutes or until lightly browned. Remove from oven and drizzle pizza sauce on top with a sprinkle of Parmesan.

SUN Chicken Noodle Soup

A hearty bowl of chicken and noodles is like medicine for your soul.

INGREDIENTS

1 pound boneless, skinless chicken breasts

1 onion, chopped

1 (10 ounce) can cream of chicken soup

1 (14 ounce) can creamed corn

2 cups chicken stock

Salt and pepper

1 (10 ounce) package frozen vegetable medley (carrots and peas work great)

1 pound small pasta (I use elbow noodles)

Parsley for garnish, chopped

In a slow cooker, place the chicken, onion, soup, creamed corn, stock, and a hearty pinch of salt and pepper. Cover and cook on low for 6 to 8 hours or on high for 3 to 4 hours. About 30 minutes before you're ready to eat, remove the lid and shred the chicken right inside the slow cooker using two forks. Next, stir in the vegetables and pasta. Cover and cook on high for another 20 to 30 minutes. Remove the lid and ladle the soup into bowls with a garnish of parsley.

 SWEET TREAT

Pumpkin Spice Latte Cake

When asked to name my favorite Bundt cake, I always say this one. It is fall. And fall is my favorite time of year.

INGREDIENTS

1 box spice cake mix

2 small boxes instant vanilla pudding

½ cup vegetable oil

1¼ cups water

4 eggs

1 cup pumpkin

4 cups powdered sugar

½ cup butter, softened

3 to 4 splashes milk

2 tablespoons cinnamon

Preheat oven to 350 degrees and grease a 10-inch Bundt pan. In mixing bowl, combine cake mix, puddings, oil, water, eggs, and pumpkin with an electric mixer. Pour into prepared Bundt pan. Bake 40 to 45 minutes, or until toothpick inserted comes out clean. Let cake rest on counter in pan 10 minutes. Invert cake onto a serving plate to finish cooling.

In a small bowl, combine powdered sugar, butter, and milk with an electric mixer until creamy. Stir in cinnamon. Frost cooled cake.

Week 4 Meal Plan

MON	Beef and Rice Skillet Supper
TUE	Chicken Tacos with Cranberry Salsa
WED	Pumpkin Rigatoni
THU	Mini BBQ Turkey Meatloaves
FRI	Apple Cheddar Turkey Burgers
SAT	Pumpkin and Sausage Ravioli Bake
SUN	Mexican Minestrone
SWEET TREAT	Rustic Apple Cranberry Pie

Shopping List

🛍 PRODUCE

1 red bell pepper
1 green bell pepper
2 onions
3 red onions
1½ cups corn (fresh or frozen)
1 bunch cilantro
2½ cups fresh cranberries
1 jalapeño
1 orange
2 garlic cloves
1 cup cubed and cooked pumpkin
Basil leaves (garnish)
8 to 10 green onions
1 shallot
Fresh chives (garnish)
1 cup grated apple (I use Fuji)
1 head romaine lettuce

🍖 MEATS

1 pound ground beef
3 pounds ground turkey
1 pound chicken
12 slices bacon
1 pound chicken breasts

🥫 CANNED FOODS, CONDIMENTS, SOUPS, SAUCES

1 (15 ounce) can black beans
1 (15 ounce) can Great Northern beans
1 (15 ounce) can pumpkin (I use Libby's)
1 (8 ounce) can tomato sauce
2 (10 ounce) cans Ro-Tel tomatoes
1 (10 ounce) can cream of chicken soup
4 cups chicken stock
Poultry seasoning
1 teaspoon garlic powder
Dijon mustard

🍞 GRAINS, PASTA, BREAD

4 cups cooked rice (I use brown rice)
6 taco shells
1 pound rigatoni
2 (9 ounce) packages sausage-filled ravioli
2 cups short-cut pasta (I use a mix of penne and shells)
Burger buns (enough to feed your family)

🍦 FROZEN

1 (10 ounce) package frozen spinach
1½ cups frozen corn

🍳 BAKING

2 cups panko breadcrumbs or breadcrumbs
⅔ cup brown sugar
1 uncooked pie crust (store-bought or homemade)
1 (21 ounce) can apple pie filling
1 tablespoon cinnamon

🍼 DAIRY

1 cup shredded Cheddar cheese (plus extra for garnish)
1 cup shredded Monterey Jack cheese
1½ cups grated Parmesan cheese
4 thick slices sharp Cheddar cheese (I use white Cheddar)
6 tablespoons half-and-half, cream, or milk
2 eggs

MON Beef and Rice Skillet Supper

This little recipe is a *big hit* at our house. It's super simple to whip up with easy cleanup too. Bonus: It's a one-pound recipe, which means if you prefer ground turkey to ground beef, just swap it out.

INGREDIENTS

1 pound ground beef

Extra virgin olive oil

Salt and pepper

1½ tablespoons cumin

1 teaspoon garlic powder

2 tablespoons Worcestershire sauce

1 red bell pepper, chopped

1 green bell pepper, chopped

1 onion, chopped

1 (8 ounce) can tomato sauce

1 (10 ounce) can Ro-Tel tomatoes (or diced tomatoes if you can't find Ro-Tel)

4 cups rice, cooked and ready to eat rice (we use brown rice)

1½ cups frozen or fresh corn

1 cup Cheddar cheese, shredded

Cilantro for garnish, chopped (optional)

In a large skillet over medium-high heat, brown the ground beef in a drizzle of olive oil. Once browned and crumbly, add in a big pinch of salt and pepper followed by the cumin and garlic powder. Next, stir in Worcestershire sauce followed by bell pepper, onion, tomato sauce, and tomatoes.

Reduce the heat to medium-low and stir everything together and allow to simmer 5 to 8 minutes. Stir the rice into the skillet along with the corn. Next, sprinkle the cheese across the top and give it just a minute to begin to melt. Remove from the heat and sprinkle with cilantro before serving.

TUE Chicken Tacos with Cranberry Salsa

Cranberries are tart and just a little sweet and pair beautifully with spicy jalapeños. Fresh and flavorful, cranberry salsa is the perfect topping to these creamy chicken tacos.

INGREDIENTS

1 cup fresh cranberries, lightly chopped

1 red onion, chopped

A handful of cilantro, chopped (you can use parsley if you don't care for cilantro)

1 jalapeño, chopped (remove the ribs and seeds for less heat)

Zest and juice of one orange (about two tablespoons zest and ½ cup juice)

1 pound Perfect Chicken, cooked and shredded (see page 6)

1 (10 ounce) box frozen spinach, thawed and all excess water squeezed out

1 (10 ounce) can cream of chicken soup

½ tablespoon chili powder

1 cup Monterey Jack cheese, shredded

Salt and pepper

6 taco shells (I like the stand-and-stuff version for baking)

Preheat the oven to 400 degrees. Grease an 8 x 8-inch baking dish (I use Pam). Set aside.

In a small bowl, combine the cranberries, onion, cilantro, jalapeño, and zest and juice from the orange. Stir everything together and refrigerate until you're ready to enjoy.

Meanwhile, in a large mixing bowl, combine the chicken, spinach, soup, chili powder, cheese, and a pinch of salt and pepper. Next, fill each taco shell with the chicken mixture and then stand the taco shell up in the prepared baking dish. Bake 8 to 10 minutes.

Remove and serve with the cranberry salsa.

WED Pumpkin Rigatoni

If you've never had pumpkin in a savory dish before, you've been missing out. Pumpkin pairs perfectly with savory suppers—especially pasta suppers! Pumpkin, bacon, Parmesan... Hello, fall!

INGREDIENTS

1 pound rigatoni

12 slices bacon

2 garlic cloves, chopped

1 red onion, chopped

1 cup chicken stock

1 cup pumpkin (not pumpkin pie filling), cubed and cooked

3 tablespoons half-and-half, cream, or milk

Freshly grated Parmesan cheese

Handful of chopped basil

Extra virgin olive oil

Salt and pepper

Bring one large pot of water to a boil for the pasta. Drop pasta in and cook 5 to 7 minutes until al dente.

In another large skillet, heat a tablespoon of olive oil over medium-high heat. Place bacon in pan and crisp both sides. Once crispy, remove bacon to a paper towel to drain. Add onion and garlic to the bacon drippings in the skillet and sauté 4 to 5 minutes. Once onion is sautéed, pour in chicken stock to deglaze your pan. Lower heat to low and let chicken stock simmer 2 to 3 minutes. Stir in pumpkin and heat through for about 3 minutes.

Meanwhile, break bacon into bite-sized pieces. Set aside.

Drain pasta and add to pumpkin mixture. Stir in half-and-half and Parmesan. Finally, add back in crispy bacon pieces and basil.

Remove from skillet, ladle pasta into bowls, and serve with a little more Parmesan and basil.

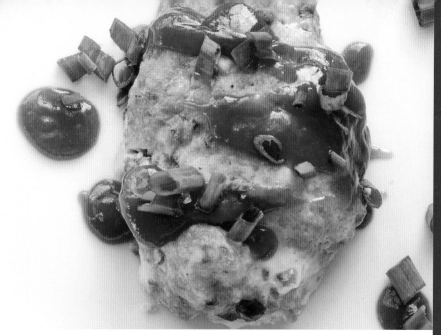

THU Mini BBQ Turkey Meatloaves

If I made my mom's meatloaf recipe every night of the week, my husband wouldn't complain. Over the years I've tweaked it into meatballs, sloppy joes, and even burgers because I'm always thinking of ways to mix and match his favorite dish. When I made a turkey version, my hubby and kiddos were all happy eaters. This recipe makes five mini meatloaves. (Add 30 minutes baking time to make one big loaf.)

INGREDIENTS

1 pound ground turkey

1 cup panko or breadcrumbs

2 eggs, beaten

6 to 8 green onions, chopped
(reserve a few for garnish)

1 teaspoon salt

5 tablespoons Worcestershire sauce, divided

1½ cups ketchup, divided

⅔ cup brown sugar

1 teaspoon mustard

Preheat the oven to 350 degrees.

Line a baking sheet with foil for easy cleanup and lightly spray with cooking spray. Set aside.

Mix the ground turkey, panko or breadcrumbs, eggs, green onions, salt, 3 tablespoons of Worcestershire sauce, and ½ cup ketchup in a bowl. Shape the mixture into 4 or 5 mini meatloaves and place them on the prepared baking sheet. Bake them in the oven for about 20 minutes.

While the meatloaves are baking, combine the remaining 2 tablespoons of Worcestershire sauce, 1 cup ketchup, the brown sugar, and the mustard in a bowl. Once 20 minutes is up, top each meatloaf with sauce and return them to the oven for 5 to 10 more minutes.

Remove from the oven, garnish with a few more green onions, and serve.

FRI Apple Cheddar Turkey Burgers

In the fall, apples and sharp Cheddar go hand in hand. Whip up a burger and make these ingredients the stars of the show along with some sautéed red onion.

INGREDIENTS

Extra virgin olive oil

1 tablespoon poultry seasoning

1 cup grated apple (I grate 1 Fuji apple with my cheese grater)

2 pounds ground turkey

4 thick slices sharp Cheddar cheese (I use white Cheddar)

1 red onion, chopped

Salt and pepper

Dijon mustard

Romaine lettuce

4 burger buns

Preheat an outdoor grill or indoor grill pan to medium-high heat.

Add 2 tablespoons of olive oil, poultry seasoning, and grated apple to the ground turkey. Divide the turkey mixture into four sections and make four patties. Grill the patties about 8 minutes per side or until cooked through. About a minute before you pull them off the grill, add a slice of cheese to each patty.

Meanwhile, sauté the red onion in a drizzle of olive oil with a big pinch of salt and pepper. Sauté until nice and tender (5 to 8 minutes).

Add the cooked burger patty to a burger bun that has been topped with romaine and then top with sautéed red onion and a nice dollop of Dijon mustard.

SAT Pumpkin and Sausage Ravioli Bake

I love, love, love pumpkin in a savory recipe—especially paired with sausage and Parmesan cheese. You can either use a store-bought sausage ravioli or substitute a cheese-filled ravioli for a vegetarian supper.

INGREDIENTS

2 (9 ounce) packages sausage-filled ravioli

1 shallot, chopped

Extra virgin olive oil

Salt and pepper

1 (15 ounce) can pumpkin (I use Libby's)

1 cup chicken stock (use veggie stock if making this vegetarian)

A splash of half-and-half, cream, or milk

1 cup Parmesan cheese, grated

1 cup breadcrumbs or panko breadcrumbs

Chives for garnish, chopped

Preheat the oven to 400 degrees. Lightly spray an 8 x 8-inch baking dish with cooking spray. Set aside.

Bring a large pot of water to a boil and drop in ravioli to cook (only 4 minutes).

Meanwhile, in a large skillet over medium-high heat, sauté the shallot in a drizzle of olive oil and a pinch of salt and pepper for a few minutes. Stir in the pumpkin and stock, add another pinch of salt and pepper, and reduce the heat to low.

After 4 minutes, drain the ravioli and then add it to the pumpkin mixture. Stir in a splash of half-and-half, cream, or milk. Pour the ravioli mixture into the prepared baking dish. Sprinkle the cheese and breadcrumbs over the top and bake 10 minutes or until lightly browned and bubbly.

Remove from oven and serve with a sprinkle of chives.

Mexican Minestrone

SUN

I'm always thinking of ways to make different versions of soups at our house. In the fall and winter, you'll find us eating soup at least twice a week for supper. This is a south-of-the-border take on a traditional Italian soup.

INGREDIENTS

1 pound chicken breasts, frozen or thawed

1 (15 ounce) can black beans, drained and rinsed

1 (15 ounce) can Great Northern beans, drained and rinsed

2 cups chicken stock

1 (10 ounce) can Ro-Tel tomatoes, undrained

1 onion, chopped

2 tablespoons chili powder or 1 packet of taco seasoning

1½ cups frozen corn

2 cups short-cut pasta (I used a mix of penne and shells for fun), uncooked

Chopped green onion and/or Cheddar cheese to garnish

In your slow cooker, combine chicken, rinsed and drained beans, chicken stock, tomatoes, onion, and chili powder. Cover and cook on low 6 to 8 hours or on high 3 to 4 hours. About 30 minutes before serving, remove lid and shred chicken right inside the slow cooker using two forks. Stir in frozen corn and pasta. Replace lid, turn the slow cooker to high, and cook another 30 minutes or so.

Ladle soup into bowls and garnish with chopped green onion and/or Cheddar cheese.

Rustic Apple Cranberry Pie

SWEET TREAT

Cranberries are so good in pancakes, muffins, cocktails, and desserts. They're tart, they're bright, and they're totally perfect for the fall. This little pie has only four ingredients. Four! Make this tonight and enjoy it in cozy socks in front of the TV.

INGREDIENTS

1 uncooked pie crust (I use a store-bought one, but you can also use homemade)

1 (21 ounce) can apple pie filling

1½ cups fresh cranberries

1 tablespoon cinnamon

Preheat the oven to 425 degrees.

Roll out the pie crust onto a lightly greased baking sheet. Set aside.

In a mixing bowl, toss the apple pie filling and cranberries together with the cinnamon. Spoon this fruit mixture into the center of the pie crust. Fold up the edges around the crust as pictured.

Pop the pie into the oven and bake 10 to 12 minutes. Remove from oven and serve immediately (maybe with some ice cream too!).

Note: Cranberries are a little tart, so if you want to sweeten them up a bit, toss them with 1 tablespoon of sugar about 10 minutes before you start assembling.

WEEK 4

Fall Notes

Winter

Week 1 Meal Plan

MON	Beef Enchiladas
TUE	Turkey and Cranberry Quesadillas
WED	Spaghetti and Meat Sauce
THU	Mom's Meatloaf
FRI	French Onion Joes
SAT	Beef and Pepper Ragu over Polenta
SUN	Spinach and Chicken Noodle Soup
SWEET TREAT	Cherry Berry Cobbler

Shopping List

PRODUCE
7 onions
3 to 4 green onions
1 pint cherry tomatoes
2 bell peppers
6 cloves garlic
Fresh basil (garnish)
Parsley (garnish)

MEATS
3 pounds ground beef
Sliced turkey (for however many sandwiches you are making)
1 pound ground beef or turkey
1½ pounds chopped flank steak or flatiron steak
1 pound boneless, skinless chicken breasts

CANNED FOODS, CONDIMENTS, SOUPS, SAUCES
1 (4 ounce) can chopped black olives
1 (10 ounce) can cream of mushroom soup
1 (10 ounce) can enchilada sauce
1 (14 ounce) can cranberry sauce
1 (28 ounce) can whole peeled tomatoes
2 (8 ounce) cans tomato sauce
1 (6 ounce) can tomato paste
1 (14 ounce) can diced tomatoes
3 cups beef stock
1 tablespoon Dijon mustard
3 cups chicken stock
2 (10 ounce) cans cream of chicken soup

GRAINS, PASTA, BREAD
1 pound spaghetti noodles
2 cups uncooked short-cut pasta (shells, rigatoni, and penne all work)
6 to 8 tortillas
Burrito-sized flour tortillas (enough to feed your family)
1 cup saltine cracker crumbs
Sourdough bread, sliced thick (1 slice per serving)

FROZEN
1 (10 ounce) package frozen spinach
1 (10 ounce) package frozen mixed berries

BAKING
⅔ cup brown sugar
1 (21 ounce) can cherry pie filling
1 (15.25 ounce) box yellow cake mix

DAIRY
2 cups shredded Cheddar cheese (plus extra for garnish)
Thick slices of cheese (1 slice for each serving)
½ cup grated Parmesan cheese
2 cups shredded Gruyere cheese
2 eggs
Ice cream (optional)

MON Beef Enchiladas

These enchiladas are delicious—and they are so simple too! These are a huge hit at our house, and it's a great dish for a potluck supper or freezer meal.

INGREDIENTS

1 pound ground beef

1 onion, chopped

1 (4 ounce) can chopped black olives, drained (optional)

2 cups Cheddar cheese, shredded

6 to 8 tortillas (flour or whole wheat)

1 (10 ounce) can cream of mushroom soup

1 (10 ounce) can enchilada sauce

Preheat oven to 350 degrees. Lightly spray an 8 x 8-inch baking dish with cooking spray; set aside.

In a large skillet over medium-high heat, cook ground beef until brown and crumbly; drain fat. Stir in chopped onion and sauté another 4 to 5 minutes. Add olives and ¾ of the cheese and stir until everything is melted together. Take each tortilla and spoon some of the cheesy ground beef mixture down the center. Roll up and place seam side down in prepared baking dish.

In a small bowl, combine mushroom soup and enchilada sauce together with a spoon. Pour this mixture over enchiladas in the pan. Sprinkle remaining cheese over the enchiladas. Bake 30 to 40 minutes or until bubbly. Remove from oven and serve.

TUE · Turkey and Cranberry Quesadillas

This is for just in case you need a recipe for Thanksgiving leftovers. You can make as many of these as you want...and you can even make just one!

INGREDIENTS

Burrito-sized flour tortillas
Turkey
Cranberry sauce

A few thick slices of cheese
(I use white Cheddar)
Green onions, chopped

Preheat an indoor griddle or a big skillet to medium-high heat. Spray lightly with cooking spray.

Lay out the tortillas. Place some turkey across the bottom half of each one. Add a big dollop of cranberry sauce, a few slices of cheese, and a few green onions to each one. Fold the top part to cover the bottom portion.

Place each quesadilla in your skillet one at a time. Brown 4 minutes or so on each side. Once they are browned, remove and slice in half (to give you two quesadillas). Repeat with your other tortillas.

WED Spaghetti and Meat Sauce

Does any meal say family supper more than spaghetti and meat sauce? You can use either ground beef or ground turkey in this recipe. Simple and satisfying!

INGREDIENTS

1 pint cherry tomatoes

Extra virgin olive oil

Salt and pepper

1 pound spaghetti noodles

1 pound ground beef or turkey

1 onion, chopped

3 cloves garlic, chopped

1 (28 ounce) can whole peeled tomatoes

1 tablespoon Italian seasoning

Parmesan cheese and basil to garnish (optional)

Preheat oven to 425 degrees. On a foil-lined baking sheet, spread cherry tomatoes out. Drizzle olive oil over the tomatoes and sprinkle liberally with salt and pepper. Roast in the oven about 15 minutes. (You can omit this step if you like and just add an extra can of tomatoes into your meat sauce, but I love the added flavor of the roasted tomatoes.)

Over medium-high heat, bring a large pot of water to a boil; add noodles and cook until al dente (about 8 minutes).

Meanwhile, over medium-high heat, brown ground beef or turkey in a skillet with a drizzle of olive oil and some salt and pepper. Once browned and crumbly, drain fat and then add onions and garlic and sauté a couple of minutes. Turn heat to low and add the can of whole, peeled tomatoes and Italian seasoning. With a wooden spoon, gently break up the whole tomatoes in the skillet. At this time, add the roasted cherry tomatoes and gently break them up too.

I like to stir a little basil and Parmesan right into my meat sauce, but you could wait and use them as a garnish instead. Drain the pasta and add to meat sauce. Serve with a sprinkle of Parmesan and a little basil.

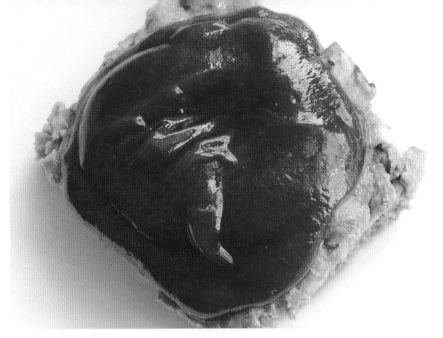

THU *Mom's Meatloaf*

This is my husband's favorite meal. Period. Favorite. It can be prepared in advance and popped in the oven at the last minute, and you probably already have all of the ingredients on hand. Served with a side of mashed potatoes, this is a man's dinner. A real man's dinner.

INGREDIENTS

1 pound ground beef

1 cup saltine cracker crumbs (about 12 crackers)

2 eggs, beaten

1 onion, chopped

1 teaspoon salt

5 tablespoons Worcestershire sauce, divided

1 (8 ounce) can tomato sauce

1 cup ketchup

$\frac{2}{3}$ cup brown sugar

1 teaspoon mustard

Preheat oven to 350 degrees. Mix ground beef, cracker crumbs, eggs, onion, salt, 3 tablespoons Worcestershire sauce, and tomato sauce in a bowl. Put in a greased 8 x 8-inch baking dish and bake 40 minutes.

Meanwhile, combine remaining 2 tablespoons Worcestershire sauce, ketchup, brown sugar, and mustard in a bowl. Once 40 minutes is up, top meatloaf with sauce and return to oven for an additional 15 minutes.

FRI French Onion Joes

It's a sloppy joe that tastes like French Onion Soup. Basically, it's perfect.

INGREDIENTS

1 pound ground beef

Extra virgin olive oil

Salt and pepper

2 onions, chopped

3 cups beef stock

1 tablespoon Dijon mustard

3 tablespoons Worcestershire sauce

Sourdough bread, sliced thick

2 cups Gruyere cheese, shredded

Parsley for garnish, chopped

In a large skillet over medium-high heat, brown the ground beef in a drizzle of olive oil. Once browned, add a big pinch of both salt and pepper before transferring the meat to a slow cooker. Next, add the onions, beef stock, Dijon, and Worcestershire sauce. Cover with a lid and cook on low for 6 to 8 hours or on high for 3 to 4 hours.

About 15 minutes before you're ready to eat, preheat oven to 425 degrees. On a baking sheet, lay out four slices of sourdough bread. Remove the lid from your slow cooker and ladle a generous portion of the ground beef on top of each piece of bread. Sprinkle with cheese and bake for about 10 minutes or until the cheese is nice and melted. Remove from the oven and garnish with parsley before serving.

SAT Beef and Pepper Ragu over Polenta

This supper is not only super simple to pull together, it's versatile too. I like to slice up firm polenta and make little corn cakes to serve with my ragu. Have fun mixing and matching ingredients.

INGREDIENTS

$1\frac{1}{2}$ pounds flank steak or flatiron steak, chopped into bite-sized pieces

Extra virgin olive oil

Salt and pepper

2 bell peppers, chopped
(I use one red and one green)

1 onion, chopped

3 cloves garlic, chopped

1 (6 ounce) can tomato paste

1 (8 ounce) can tomato sauce

1 (14 ounce) can diced tomatoes (do not drain)

Parmesan cheese, grated

In a large skillet over medium-high heat, brown the steak in a drizzle of olive oil along with a pinch of salt and pepper.

Once browned, add the bell peppers, onion, and garlic along with another pinch of salt and pepper and sauté about 5 minutes or until the veggies are tender. Stir in the tomato paste, tomato sauce, and diced tomatoes. Reduce the heat to low and simmer 10 minutes.

Remove from the heat and ladle the ragu over polenta or any other carb you love (pasta would be great!). Garnish with a little grated Parmesan cheese.

Spinach and Chicken Noodle Soup

I'm such a sucker for a good bowl of soup. I make this one in the slow cooker so my house smells yummy all day. Warm. Hearty. Comforting. Soup.

INGREDIENTS

3 cups chicken stock

1 onion, chopped

2 (10 ounce) cans cream of chicken soup

1 (10 ounce) package of frozen spinach, thawed and all excess water squeezed out

Salt and pepper

1 pound boneless, skinless chicken breasts (uncooked)

2 cups uncooked short-cut pasta (shells, rigatoni, and penne all work)

Shredded Cheddar cheese to garnish

In your slow cooker, layer the first 6 ingredients. Cover and cook on low 6 to 7 hours or on high about 3 hours.

About 30 minutes before you're ready to eat, remove the lid, shred the chicken right inside the slow cooker using two forks, and pour pasta in. Cover and continue to cook about 30 minutes or until the noodles are tender. Try not to remove the lid during that 30 minutes or it will take your noodles a lot longer to cook.

When the noodles are cooked, ladle into bowls and garnish with a little cheese.

SWEET TREAT *Cherry Berry Cobbler*

I just cannot stop making this cobbler. It's simple to make and delicious every time. After a special meal, enjoy this delicious cobbler with the ones you love.

INGREDIENTS

1 (10 ounce) package frozen mixed berries (do not thaw)

1 (21 ounce) can cherry pie filling

1 (15.25 ounce) yellow cake mix

½ cup butter, melted

Ice cream, optional

Preheat oven to 350 degrees and grease a 9 x 13-inch baking dish. Spread frozen berries across bottom of dish. Next, spoon pie filling on top of the frozen berries, and then sprinkle the box of dry cake mix over the pie filling. Finally, drizzle the melted butter over everything.

Bake uncovered 55 to 60 minutes. Remove from oven and serve immediately (with a little ice cream if you desire). I promise...you'll make it once and then make it over and over again.

Week 2 Meal Plan

MON	Beefy Cornbread Casserole
TUE	Baked Queso Tacos
WED	Creamy Tomato Chicken Pasta
THU	Saucy Cranberry Meatballs
FRI	Italian Brisket Sandwiches
SAT	Meatball Stroganoff
SUN	Andrea's Baked Potato Soup
SWEET TREAT	Butterfinger Blondies

Shopping List

 PRODUCE
4 onions
20 to 22 green onions
3 cloves garlic
4 large russet potatoes
Basil leaves (garnish)

 MEATS
1 pound ground beef, chicken, or turkey
2½ pounds ground beef
1 pound chicken breasts
1 (1 pound) bag frozen meatballs (I use Italian-style chicken meatballs)
1 (3 to 5 pounds) brisket
12 slices cooked bacon

CANNED FOODS, CONDIMENTS, SOUPS, SAUCES
1 (10 ounce) can Ro-Tel tomatoes
1 (14 ounce) can diced tomatoes
1 (28 ounce) can whole peeled tomatoes
1 (8 ounce) can tomato sauce
1 (14 ounce) can whole berry cranberry sauce
1 (9 ounce) bottle hoisin sauce
1 (10 ounce) can cream of mushroom soup
1 (10 ounce) can tomato soup
1 teaspoon garlic powder
1 (1 ounce) packet powdered Italian dressing mix
1 cup beef stock
3 cups chicken stock

 GRAINS, PASTA, BREAD
8 taco shells
1 pound pasta
Cooked white rice (enough to feed your family)
Burger buns (enough to feed your family)

 FROZEN
1 (10 ounce) package frozen spinach
1 (10 ounce) package frozen mixed berries

BAKING
¼ cup brown sugar plus 1 tablespoon
3 cups powdered sugar
1 (8 ounce) package cornbread mix (I use Jiffy)
¼ cup breadcrumbs or panko breadcrumbs
1 (15.25 ounce) box yellow cake mix
5 regular-sized Butterfingers

DAIRY
1 (8 ounce) package Velveeta cheese
4 ounces cream cheese
½ cup grated Parmesan cheese
2 cups grated Cheddar cheese
2½ cups sour cream
5 eggs
7 cups milk

Beefy Cornbread Casserole

This is just one of those feel-good suppers. It's a simple and hearty dinner for your family!

INGREDIENTS

1 pound ground beef, chicken, or turkey

1 onion, chopped

1½ cups ketchup

¼ cup brown sugar

2 tablespoons Worcestershire sauce

1 tablespoon chili powder

1 (8 ounce) package cornbread mix (I use Jiffy)

½ cup milk

1 egg

Sour cream and/or shredded Cheddar cheese to garnish

Preheat oven to 350 degrees. Grease an 8 x 8-inch baking dish and set aside. In a large skillet over medium-high heat, brown ground beef and onion until cooked and crumbly; drain fat. Stir in the next 4 ingredients and reduce heat to low. Simmer together about 5 minutes and then pour beef mixture into prepared baking dish.

In a small bowl, mix dry cornbread mix with milk and egg. Pour batter over ground beef mixture. Bake uncovered about 20 minutes or until cornbread is browned on the edges and the casserole is bubbly. Remove from oven and let stand 5 minutes before cutting into squares and garnishing with sour cream and/or shredded cheese.

This recipe serves 4 adults but could be easily doubled and prepared in a 9 x 13-inch baking dish.

TUE *Baked Queso Tacos*

Combine tacos with creamy queso cheese sauce and then bake them in the oven...yes! Not only are these tacos super simple to whip up, but they're also freakin' awesome. That's right, I called a taco freakin' awesome...because it is.

INGREDIENTS

1½ pounds ground beef

Extra virgin olive oil

Salt and pepper

1 (8 ounce) package Velveeta cheese

1 (10 ounce) can Ro-Tel tomatoes

1½ tablespoons chili powder

Green onions for garnish, chopped

8 taco shells (I use the stand-and-stuff variety because they're easier to bake)

Preheat oven to 400 degrees. Grease an 8 x 8-inch baking dish (I use Pam). Set aside.

In a skillet over medium-high heat, brown the ground beef in a drizzle of olive oil. Once browned and crumbly, add a pinch of salt and pepper. Next, stir in the Velveeta, tomatoes, and chili powder. Stir everything together until the cheese is melted.

Take each taco shell and fill it with the ground beef mixture. Place the tacos in the prepared baking dish until all of the taco shells and baking dish are filled. Pop the dish in the oven (about 8 minutes to brown). Remove from the oven and serve immediately with chopped green onions on top.

Creamy Tomato Chicken Pasta

I think the key to a good slow cooker meal is adding a little freshness at the end. The grated cheese and fresh basil really brighten up this supper. Sometimes, I'll cook the pasta in the slow cooker, but in this recipe I really don't want the pasta to absorb all of the sauce, so I cook up the pasta right before serving.

INGREDIENTS

1 pound uncooked chicken breasts (frozen or thawed)

1 cup chicken stock (or water)

1 (1 ounce) packet powdered Italian dressing mix

1 onion, chopped

1 (10 ounce) can tomato soup

1 (14 ounce) can diced tomatoes

4 ounces cream cheese (half a block)

$1/2$ pound pasta, cooked

Grated Parmesan cheese to garnish

Fresh basil to garnish

In your slow cooker, combine chicken, stock, packet of dry seasoning mix, onion, tomato soup, and diced tomatoes. Cover and cook on low 6 to 8 hours or on high about 3 hours.

Half an hour before serving, remove lid and shred the chicken right inside the slow cooker using two forks. Turn the heat to high and add cream cheese. Replace the lid and cook on high the last 30 minutes.

Right before you serve, add the hot, cooked pasta to the slow cooker and stir everything together. Ladle pasta into bowls and garnish with some grated Parmesan and fresh basil.

THU Saucy Cranberry Meatballs

These meatballs are a *must* this holiday season. Only three ingredients are required. If you haven't had hoisin sauce, it's kind of like an Asian BBQ sauce. Trust me, you'll like it!

INGREDIENTS

1 (1 pound) bag frozen meatballs (we use Italian-style chicken meatballs)

1 (14 ounce) can whole berry cranberry sauce

1 (9 ounce) bottle hoisin sauce (found on the international food aisle)

Cooked white rice (if you're serving as an entree)

Green onions, chopped (if you're serving as an entree)

Place the meatballs, cranberry sauce, and hoisin sauce in a slow cooker. Cover and cook on low for 6 to 8 hours or on high for 3 to 4 hours.

If you're serving the meatballs as an entree, you can plate some cooked and fluffy rice to go under them and garnish with a few chopped green onions. If you're serving the meatballs as an appetizer, you're done!

FRI Italian Brisket Sandwiches

Brisket is such an easy cut of meat to cook in the slow cooker, so we eat it often...especially during the fall and winter. These open-faced sandwiches are super simple and really yummy!

INGREDIENTS

1 (3 to 5 pounds) brisket

Extra virgin olive oil

Salt and pepper

2 tablespoons Italian seasoning

1 onion, chopped

3 cloves garlic (leave whole)

1 (28 ounce) can whole peeled tomatoes

1 cup beef stock, chicken stock, or water

1 (8 ounce) can tomato sauce

1 tablespoon brown sugar

1 tablespoon Worcestershire sauce

Burger buns

Grated Parmesan cheese to garnish

Basil to garnish

In a large pan over medium-high heat, brown both sides of the brisket in a tablespoon of oil, about 3 minutes per side. Sprinkle salt and pepper liberally over each side.

Once browned, put brisket in slow cooker. Sprinkle Italian seasoning over the brisket and add onion, whole garlic cloves, can of whole tomatoes, and stock (or water). Cover and cook on high about 8 hours.

An hour before you're ready to eat, combine tomato sauce, brown sugar, and Worcestershire sauce in a small bowl. Set aside. Remove brisket from the slow cooker to a cutting board; drain everything out of the slow cooker. Return the brisket to the hot slow cooker and shred it up using two forks. Pour tomato sauce mixture over everything, cover, and continue cooking another 30 minutes to 1 hour.

When you're ready to serve, top each bun with some of the shredded brisket, a sprinkle of Parmesan, and some basil.

SAT *Meatball Stroganoff*

Meatballs are a huge hit in our family. And doesn't everyone love pasta? I combined the two, and my family went nuts for this recipe. Simple, quick, and yummy.

INGREDIENTS

1 pound ground beef

$\frac{1}{2}$ an onion, grated (just use a cheese grater)

2 tablespoons Worcestershire sauce, divided

$\frac{1}{2}$ cup breadcrumbs or panko breadcrumbs

2 eggs, lightly beaten

1 tablespoon butter

1 tablespoon flour

1 (10 ounce) can cream of mushroom soup

2 cups chicken stock

1 teaspoon garlic powder

Salt and pepper

2 tablespoons sour cream (or a little more if you like)

$\frac{1}{2}$ pound cooked pasta for serving

Green onions for garnish, chopped

Preheat the oven to 400 degrees. Line a baking sheet in foil and lightly spray with Pam. Set aside.

In a large mixing bowl, combine the ground beef, onion, 1 tablespoon of Worcestershire sauce, breadcrumbs, and eggs. Form into small meatballs. (I make 18 small meatballs.) Place the meatballs on the prepared baking sheet and bake 15 minutes or until browned.

While the meatballs are baking, heat the butter over medium-high heat in a large skillet. Quickly whisk the flour into the melted butter and whisk about a minute. Stir in the mushroom soup, remaining tablespoon of Worcestershire sauce, and stock and bring to a gentle boil. Then reduce heat to low. Stir in the garlic powder and a nice pinch of salt and pepper.

Remove the meatballs from the oven and add them to your skillet mixture. Simmer about 10 minutes, stirring them around often. Right before serving, stir in the sour cream.

Serve the meatballs and sauce over cooked noodles. Sprinkle with green onions if desired.

SUN Andrea's Baked Potato Soup

When my family was eating at my bestie Andrea's house, we were served this amazing Baked Potato Soup. I'm going to declare it the best Baked Potato Soup I've ever had. Ever. And it's easy to make too. Win, win.

INGREDIENTS

²/₃ cup butter

²/₃ cup flour

6 cups milk (I use 2%)

4 large russet potatoes, baked and the insides scooped out

12 slices bacon, cooked and chopped, with some reserved for garnish (we use turkey bacon)

12 green onions, chopped, with some rerserved for garnish

1½ cups Cheddar cheese, grated and divided

1 cup sour cream

Salt and pepper

Melt the butter in a large soup pot over medium-high heat. Once melted, whisk in the flour and stir about a minute. Slowly pour in the milk and continue to whisk. Whisk constantly until it thickens and is a little bubbly. (It only took about 10 minutes for mine to thicken, but it could take yours a bit longer. If you use a lot of skim milk, it will take longer.)

Once the milk is nice and thick, carefully stir in what you scooped out of the potatoes, most of the bacon (reserving some for garnish), most of the green onions (reserving some for garnish), and one cup of Cheddar cheese. Add a generous pinch of salt and pepper.

Stir everything together until the cheese is nice and melted, and then stir in the sour cream.

Ladle the soup into bowls and garnish with remaining pieces of bacon, cheese, and green onions.

SWEET TREAT *Butterfinger Blondies*

These are just fabulous. I mixed and matched my favorite bar recipe and added chopped Butterfingers. Not only are these really simple, they're really yummy too!

INGREDIENTS

1 box yellow cake mix

$\frac{1}{2}$ cup vegetable oil

3 eggs

5 regular-sized Butterfingers, chopped (about 3 cups)

$\frac{1}{2}$ cup butter, softened

3 cups powdered sugar

Splash of milk

Preheat oven to 350 degrees and grease a 9 x 13-inch baking dish; set aside. In a mixing bowl, combine cake mix, vegetable oil, and eggs with an electric mixer. Stir in one cup chopped Butterfingers. Pour batter into prepared pan and bake 20 minutes or until a toothpick inserted in the middle comes out clean.

While the bars are cooling, prepare frosting. In a mixing bowl, combine butter and powdered sugar with milk. Add more powdered sugar if it's too thin or more milk if it's too thick. Once your frosting reaches the desired consistency, stir in remaining 2 cups Butterfinger candy. Top cooled bars with frosting. Refrigerate at least 2 hours before slicing and serving.

Week 3 Meal Plan

MON	Cowboy Stew
TUE	BBQ Chicken Rice Bowls
WED	Perfect Parmesan Pasta
THU	Red Beans and Rice
FRI	Steak and Wedge Burgers
SAT	Pomegranate Chicken Spinach Tacos
SUN	Beer Chicken Chili
SWEET TREAT	Hot Chocolate Cupcakes with Peppermint Buttercream Frosting

Shopping List

PRODUCE
3 onions
20 green onions
1 red onion
2 red bell peppers
2 potatoes
1½ cups corn (fresh or frozen)
2 avocados
3 cloves garlic
1½ cups fresh pomegranate seeds
1 head iceberg lettuce
1 pint cherry tomatoes
1 jalapeño pepper
Parsley (garnish)

MEATS
4 pounds ground beef
3 pounds boneless, skinless chicken breasts
1 pound chicken
1 pound sausage
14 slices bacon

CANNED FOODS, CONDIMENTS, SOUPS, SAUCES
2 cups beef stock
6 cups chicken stock
2 cans soda (I use Dr Pepper, but Coca-Cola or root beer work well too)
1 (18 ounce) bottle BBQ sauce (I love Sweet Baby Ray's)
1 (28 ounce) can peeled tomatoes
2 (14 ounce) cans diced tomatoes
1 (8 ounce) can tomato sauce
1 (12 ounce) jar candied jalapeños
2 (15 ounce) cans red kidney beans
1 (16 ounce) can chili beans
Hot pepper sauce
Steak seasoning

2 teaspoons garlic powder
Ranch dressing (for drizzling)
1 cup beer

GRAINS, PASTA, BREAD

6 cups cooked rice (I use brown rice)
1 pound penne pasta
Flour tortillas (enough to feed your family)
Burger buns (enough to feed your family)

FROZEN
1 (10 ounce) bag frozen mixed vegetables

BAKING
3 tablespoons cornstarch
1 (15.25 ounces) box chocolate cake mix
3 tablespoons instant hot chocolate powder
3 cups powdered sugar
2 teaspoons peppermint extract
Red food coloring
Peppermint crunch, candy cane marshmallows, peppermint M&M's, or candy cane Kisses (garnish)

DAIRY
2 cups grated mozzarella cheese
1 cup grated Parmesan cheese
Grated white Cheddar cheese (garnish)
Crumbled bleu cheese (topping)
Shredded Cheddar cheese (garnish)
1 (8 ounce) package cream cheese
4 eggs
1 to 2 tablespoons milk

MON Cowboy Stew

Mmm! Your house is going to smell insanely delicious while this stew is baking. That's right...
baking. You brown some ground beef, add everything else into the pot, and then bake it to
completion. It's a stew fit for a cowboy or any hungry person at your table.

INGREDIENTS

2 pounds ground beef

Extra virgin olive oil

Salt and pepper

1 onion, chopped

1 red bell pepper, chopped

2 potatoes, diced into small bites

1 (10 ounce) bag frozen vegetables (I use green
beans, peas, and corn)

2 teaspoons garlic powder

3 tablespoons Worcestershire sauce

1 (14 ounce) can diced tomatoes (do not drain)

2 cups beef stock

3 tablespoons cornstarch

3 tablespoons water

In a large, oven-safe pot, brown the ground beef in a drizzle of olive oil over medium-high heat.
Once browned and crumbly, add a big pinch of salt and pepper followed by the next 8 ingredients. Add one more pinch of salt and pepper before putting a lid on the pot and placing it in the
oven. Bake at 250 degrees for 45 minutes.

After 45 minutes, take the cornstarch and whisk it together with the water in a small bowl. Pull
the stew out of the oven just a bit, remove the lid, and stir the cornstarch mixture in. Cover and
put back in the oven another 15 to 20 minutes to finish baking. After that, remove from the oven
and you're ready to serve. The potatoes should be tender and the stew nice and thick. Ladle into
bowls and enjoy!

BBQ Chicken Rice Bowls

Bright, colorful, flavorful...this simple supper is really, really good. Like, you'll be surprised how much you love it considering how simple it is to throw it together. Another favorite for mixing and matching all of your ingredients.

INGREDIENTS

1 pound boneless, skinless chicken breasts

2 cans soda (we use Dr Pepper, but you could use cola or root beer)

1 bottle BBQ sauce (we love Sweet Baby Ray's)

½ cups corn, heated (we just microwave frozen corn)

4 cups rice, cooked and ready to eat (we use brown rice, but you can use your favorite)

2 avocados, chopped

8 green onions, chopped

Place the chicken breasts inside a slow cooker. Pour the soda on top of them, cover, and cook on low for 6 to 8 hours or on high for 3 to 4 hours.

When you're ready to eat, remove the lid, pull out the chicken, and place it in a large mixing bowl. Take two forks and shred it. Stir in as much of the BBQ sauce as you like and stir in the corn.

Add 1 cup of rice to each serving bowl and top with the BBQ chicken and corn mixture. Then top everything with the avocado and green onions.

WED Perfect Parmesan Pasta

I call this Perfect Parmesan Pasta because it's like Chicken Parmesan but in a bowl with pasta. Basically, it's perfect. Your pasta lovers will totally dig this hearty supper.

INGREDIENTS

1 pound penne pasta

1 onion, chopped

3 cloves garlic, chopped

1 (28 ounce) can peeled tomatoes

1 (8 ounce) can tomato sauce

2 tablespoons Italian seasoning blend

1 pound Perfect Chicken (see page 6)

2 cups grated Mozzarella cheese

1 cup grated Parmesan cheese

Extra virgin olive oil

Salt and pepper

Preheat oven to 425 degrees. Grease an 8 x 8-inch baking dish and set aside.

Bring a large pot of water to a boil. Drop in pasta and cook until al dente (about 7 to 8 minutes).

Meanwhile, in a large skillet over medium-high heat, heat a drizzle of olive oil and add in onion. Sauté until tender and then add garlic. Sauté another minute before adding in peeled tomatoes and tomato sauce. Break up peeled tomatoes with the back of a spoon. Stir in Italian seasoning and cooked and shredded chicken.

Drain pasta (reserve about a cup of the hot water). Add hot pasta and reserved water to skillet. Toss everything together and then pour it into prepared baking dish. Sprinkle cheeses over the top of the casserole and pop it in the oven. Bake about 15 minutes or until the cheese is melted and bubbly.

Remove from oven and serve immediately.

Red Beans and Rice

Red Beans and Rice was a staple in my house growing up. My mom made it often, and we always ate it up. It's a simple and flavorful dish that whips up in minutes. I like to use my slow cooker for this recipe, but you could also make this on the stovetop. Just let the flavors bubble together for about 30 minutes and then serve over cooked rice.

INGREDIENTS

1 pound sausage, sliced into round pieces or chopped (I use turkey but you can use pork)

2 (15 ounce) cans red kidney beans, drained

1 (14 ounce) can diced tomatoes

1 onion, chopped

Hot pepper sauce to taste (you can add more after it's done cooking...start small and build up)

Salt and pepper to taste

Red pepper flakes to taste (again, add a little bit at a time)

2 cups cooked rice (I use brown rice)

Place the first 4 ingredients in your slow cooker. Add a few dashes of hot pepper sauce and a pinch of your spices. (You can always add more at the end if you need more flavor.) Cover and cook on low for 6 to 8 hours or on high for 3 to 4 hours.

When you're ready to serve, remove the lid and ladle your mixture on top of the cooked rice.

FRI Steak and Wedge Burgers

When you find something your whole family enjoys, you make it. On repeat. Two of our family faves are combined in this one dinner: burgers and a wedge salad. A-mazing.

INGREDIENTS

2 pounds ground beef

Extra virgin olive oil

2 tablespoons steak seasoning

1 head iceberg lettuce, chopped into four big pieces (keeping the stem intact at the bottom so it doesn't come apart when you grill it)

4 burger buns

Ranch dressing to drizzle

6 pieces bacon, cooked to a crisp and then crumbled

Cherry tomatoes, quartered

1 red onion, chopped

Bleu cheese, crumbled

Preheat an outdoor grill or indoor grill pan over medium-high heat.

In a mixing bowl, combine the ground beef, a few drizzles of olive oil, and steak seasoning together. Divide this mixture and make four patties. (Make sure to press down each patty a little in the center to avoid the "burger bulge" when they grill.)

Add the burger patties to the grill and begin cooking. (We grill ours 6 minutes or so per side.) About two minutes before you're ready to remove the burgers, add the four pieces of iceberg lettuce to the grill and grill both sides. (If you leave the stem intact, the lettuce won't fall apart when you're grilling it. We grill the lettuce about a minute or two per side. Just long enough to get a smoky touch and great grill marks.)

When the patties and lettuce are done, remove from the grill and assemble burgers—bun, grilled iceberg lettuce, patty, a drizzle of ranch dressing, quartered cherry tomatoes, chopped red onion, bacon crumbles, and bleu cheese.

SAT · Pomegranate Chicken Spinach Tacos

Pomegranate seeds and December just go hand in hand. This little super food has great flavor, a nice crunch, and a fun bright color that can cheer up any cold and gray day. We eat these tacos with candied jalapeños, but if you can't find those, regular deli jalapeños will work just fine too! A little heat goes great with the pomegranate seeds.

INGREDIENTS

1 pound chicken breasts

4 cups chicken stock or water

2 tablespoons chili powder

Flour tortillas

Candied jalapeños

White Cheddar cheese, grated

1½ cups fresh pomegranate seeds

8 green onions, chopped

Place chicken breasts and stock in a slow cooker. Cook on low 6 to 8 hours or high 3 to 4 hours. When ready to serve, remove chicken from slow cooker and place it in a bowl. Take two forks and shred chicken. Stir in chili powder.

Take each tortilla and build your taco. Add candied jalapeños, white Cheddar, pomegranate seeds, and green onions.

SUN Beer Chicken Chili

This stove top chili is the perfect ending to a cozy week. Full of flavor but not a lot of work!

INGREDIENTS

1 pound chicken breasts

Extra virgin olive oil

Salt and pepper

8 slices bacon, chopped

1 red bell pepper, chopped

1 jalapño pepper, seeded and chopped

2 tablespoons chili powder

1 (16 ounce) can chili beans, undrained

1 cup beer

2 cups chicken stock

Chopped green onions to garnish

Shredded Cheddar cheese to garnish

Chop chicken into bite-sized pieces. Set aside. In a large pot over medium-high heat, drizzle in a tablespoon or so of olive oil. Add in chopped chicken and a big pinch of salt and pepper. Allow chicken to brown on both sides, about 5 minutes. Once brown, add bacon and allow to crisp.

Next, add bell pepper and jalapeño pepper and sauté 1 to 2 minutes. Add in chili powder and chili beans. Stir in beer and stock, reduce heat to medium-low, and simmer about 10 minutes, stirring occasionally.

When ready to serve, ladle into bowls and garnish with green onions and shredded cheese. That's it! The beer adds a nice depth of flavor, but the alcohol burns off and makes this a family meal.

Hot Chocolate Cupcakes

Early in the Christmas season, we love to make these yummy, festive cupcakes. They combine all the kid favorites of the season—hot chocolate, peppermint, and Christmas candy. They're the perfect little party treat for all of your merry and bright nights!

INGREDIENTS

1 box chocolate cake mix

3 tablespoons instant hot chocolate powder

½ cup vegetable oil

1¼ cups water

4 eggs

1 (8 ounce) package cream cheese, softened

3 cups powdered sugar

1 or 2 tablespoons milk

2 teaspoons peppermint extract

Red food coloring

Peppermint crunch, candy cane marshmallows, peppermint M&M's, or candy cane Kisses to garnish

Preheat the oven to 350 degrees. Line 2 (12 count) muffin tins with cupcake liners.

Combine the cake mix, hot chocolate powder, oil, water, and eggs in a mixing bowl with an electric mixer. Pour the batter into the prepared muffin tins and bake 16 to 18 minutes or until a toothpick inserted comes out clean. Let the cupcakes rest on the counter in the pan 5 minutes before removing them to a wire rack to finish cooling.

To make the frosting, beat the cream cheese, powdered sugar, and milk with an electric mixer until smooth. Add more powdered sugar if your frosting is too thin and more milk if it's too thick. Beat in the peppermint extract and a few drops of red food coloring until they are incorporated.

Frost the cooled cupcakes with the peppermint cream cheese frosting and garnish with your favorite Christmas candy.

Week 4 Meal Plan

MON	Sausage and Cabbage Skillet
TUE	Chicken Citrus Tostadas
WED	Roasted Garlic and Tomato Pasta
THU	Provolone Lasagna
FRI	Portobello Burgers
SAT	Mexican Beef over Cornbread
SUN	Pepperoni Pizza Soup
SWEET TREAT	Coconut Cream Pie

Shopping List

PRODUCE
3 cups purple cabbage
2 red onions
3 onions
12 green onions
4 bulbs garlic
4 to 5 oranges
4 cups cherry tomatoes
2 large bunches basil
2 green bell peppers
4 large portobello mushroom caps
Spinach leaves
Fresh parsley (garnish)

MEATS
1 (12 ounce) package sausage
1 pound chicken
2 pounds ground beef
2 pounds ground beef or bulk Italian sausage
1 pound stew meat (or brisket)
2 cups sliced pepperoni

CANNED FOODS, CONDIMENTS, SOUPS, SAUCES
3 tablespoons apple cider vinegar
1½ tablespoons Dijon mustard
1 cup BBQ sauce (I use Sweet Baby Ray's)
2 (28 ounce) cans whole peeled tomatoes
   (I use San Marzano)
1 (10 ounce) can Ro-Tel tomatoes
1 (28 ounce) can crushed tomatoes
1 (8 ounce) can tomato sauce
2 (6 ounce) cans tomato paste
1 cup salsa
½ cup guacamole
Pinch ground fennel seeds (optional)

GRAINS, PASTA, BREAD
1 (16.3 ounce) can refrigerated biscuits
4 to 6 tostada shells
1 pound pasta
1 box lasagna noodles
Pretzel bread (optional)
Burger buns (enough to feed your family)

FROZEN
1 (10 ounce) package frozen spinach
1 (10 ounce) package frozen mixed berries

BAKING
1 (8.5 ounce) box cornbread mix, prepared
   (or premade cornbread)
2 cups toasted coconut
1 homemade or store-bought 9-inch pie crust

DAIRY
2½ cups grated Parmesan cheese
2 shredded cups provolone cheese
Shredded cheese (garnish)
1 (4 ounce) container goat cheese
   (for spreading on burgers)
1½ cups shredded mozzarella cheese
Sour cream (garnish)
1½ cups half-and-half
1½ cups milk
2 eggs
1 (8 ounce) container Cool Whip

MON Sausage and Cabbage Skillet

Oh, friends, here is one easy skillet supper! My kiddos are big fans of any recipe that involves kielbasa (because it's basically like a big hot dog in their little eyes). I love to serve this recipe with pretzel bread from our market's bakery for a winning combination.

INGREDIENTS

1 (12 ounce) package sausage, cut into rounds

Extra virgin olive oil

3 cups purple cabbage, shredded

1 red onion, chopped

3 cloves garlic, chopped

3 tablespoons apple cider vinegar

1½ tablespoons Dijon mustard

Salt and pepper

Parsley for garnish, chopped

Pretzel bread on the side (optional)

In a large skillet over medium-high heat, brown the sausage rounds in a drizzle of olive oil for a few minutes and then add the cabbage, onion, and garlic along with a big pinch of salt and pepper. Sauté a few minutes until everything is tender.

Meanwhile, in a small bowl, whisk together the apple cider vinegar and mustard along with another little pinch of salt and pepper. After your cabbage and sausage mixture is nice and tender, stir this mixture into the skillet and toss everything together. Let the sausage and cabbage sauté another couple of minutes, and then you'll be ready to serve. Scoop a portion onto each plate and garnish with some chopped parsley and pretzel bread.

TUE *Chicken Citrus Tostadas*

'Tis the season for citrus! Winter is the perfect time to combine oranges with other flavors, so I decided to put an orange spin on a chicken tostada. So good, so easy, and so eaten up by everyone at the dinner table. You could also use corn, flour, or crunchy taco shells instead of a tostada.

INGREDIENTS

1 cup fresh orange juice (about 2 juicy oranges)

1 cup BBQ sauce (I use Sweet Baby Ray's)

1 pound Perfect Chicken (see page 6)

8 green onions, chopped

4 to 6 tostada shells

Orange slices for garnish

In a small bowl, combine the orange juice and BBQ sauce. Pour this over the chicken. Scoop out a generous portion of chicken onto each tostada shell and sprinkle a few green onions on top. Garnish with an orange wedge or two.

WEEK 4

Roasted Garlic and Tomato Pasta

The key to this supper is roasting the garlic and tomatoes before you begin. If you've never roasted garlic or tomatoes before, no worries...it's simple! A little roasting creates big flavor.

INGREDIENTS

2 garlic bulbs

Extra virgin olive oil

Salt and pepper

4 cups cherry tomatoes

1 pound ground beef

1 pound pasta (we use whole wheat linguine)

1 (28 ounce) can peeled, whole tomatoes

1 (8 ounce) can tomato sauce

Parmesan cheese for garnish, grated

Basil for garnish, chopped

Preheat the oven to 425 degrees. Line a baking sheet with foil. Set aside.

Take each bulb of garlic and cut off the top, exposing the inside but keeping the bulb intact. Drizzle with olive oil and sprinkle with salt and pepper. Wrap each bulb in foil and place on your baking sheet. Roast for 20 minutes.

After 20 minutes, add the cherry tomatoes. Drizzle with olive oil and a pinch of salt and pepper. Pop everything back in the oven and roast for another 15 minutes.

Meanwhile, brown the ground beef in a large skillet in a drizzle of olive oil. Once browned and crumbly, sprinkle in salt and pepper. While your ground beef is browning, bring water to a boil in a large pot over medium-high heat. Add the pasta and cook to al dente (7 to 8 minutes).

When the ground beef is browned, stir in tomatoes and tomato sauce. Using the back of a spoon, lightly press on the canned tomatoes to break them up a bit. Remove the cherry tomatoes and garlic from the oven. Unwrap the garlic bulbs, pull out the roasted garlic, and add it to your skillet along with cherry tomatoes. Reduce the heat to low and allow to simmer for 5 minutes.

Drain the pasta and add the hot pasta to the ground beef mixture. Toss everything to coat and serve. Garnish with Parmesan cheese and basil.

Provolone Lasagna

We have people over for supper a lot this time of year, and this is one of my favorite things to make. I love that you can make it in advance and then pop it in the oven before your guests arrive.

INGREDIENTS

2 pounds ground beef (or bulk Italian sausage)

Extra virgin olive oil

1 onion, chopped

3 cloves garlic, chopped

1 (28 ounce) can whole tomatoes

1 (6 ounce) can tomato paste

2 tablespoons Italian seasoning

A big handful of basil, chopped
  (reserve some for garnish)

1 cup of Parmesan cheese, grated
  (reserve some for garnish)

2 cups provolone cheese, shredded

1 (10 to 12 ounce) box lasagna noodles

Salt and pepper

Preheat the oven to 350 degrees. Grease a 9 x 13-inch baking dish (I use Pam). Set aside.

In a pot over medium-high heat, brown the meat in a big drizzle of olive oil. Once browned and crumbly, stir in the onion and garlic. Sauté 5 minutes or until the onions are tender. Next, stir in the whole tomatoes, lightly breaking them up with a wooden spoon or spatula. Stir in the tomato paste, Italian seasoning, basil, and Parmesan cheese. Reduce the heat to low and allow everything to simmer for 10 minutes. After that, you're ready to assemble.

Spread a third of the meat mixture across the bottom of the prepared baking dish. Next, layer a third of your provolone, followed by a row of lasagna noodles. Repeat once more. After that, spread the remaining third of your meat mixture over the lasagna noodles followed by the rest of the provolone.

Bake uncovered 35 to 40 minutes or until the edges of the noodles brown a bit and it's nice and bubbly. Remove from the oven and allow to sit 5 minutes. Garnish with Parmesan cheese and chopped basil.

FRI Portobello Burgers

Yummy! We made Portobello Burgers for dinner the other night, and they were eaten up! Lots of burger flavor without the meat. Score one for the vegetarian in you! (And *pssst...*if there's a meat lover in your family, then toss a beef patty on the grill under that mushroom and call it a day!)

INGREDIENTS

1 large red onion, chopped

Extra virgin olive oil

Salt and pepper

4 large portobello mushroom caps

Goat cheese for spreading on each burger

A handful of spinach leaves

Guacamole for topping

4 burger buns

Preheat an outdoor grill or indoor grill pan to medium-high. At the same time, heat a large skillet over medium-high heat.

Add the onion to the skillet along with a drizzle of olive oil and a nice pinch of salt and pepper. Sauté until caramelized (10 to 15 minutes).

Meanwhile, take each mushroom cap and lightly wipe it off with a slightly damp paper towel (don't clean them under running water). Dry them well and then drizzle olive oil on each one (about 1 tablespoon per cap). Place the mushroom caps on the grill and cook (4 minutes or so per side). At the end of the grilling, sprinkle salt and pepper over the mushrooms. Remove to serve.

When you're ready to assemble, take a bun, spread yummy goat cheese on top, add some spinach, a portobello mushroom, caramelized onion, and a big dollop of guacamole.

SAT · *Mexican Beef over Cornbread*

Throw stew meat in a slow cooker along with some veggies, and then scoop the goodness over yummy cornbread. Simple. Hearty. Done.

INGREDIENTS

1 pound stew meat (or you could use a brisket)

Extra virgin olive oil

1 tablespoon chili powder

Salt and pepper

1 onion, chopped

1 green bell pepper, chopped

1 (10 ounce) can Ro-Tel tomatoes

1 cup salsa

1 cup water

Cornbread, prepared

Cheese for garnish (optional)

Sour cream (optional)

Green onions for garnish, chopped (optional)

Guacamole for garnish (optional)

In a skillet over medium-high heat, brown the beef in a little olive oil a few minutes on each side (just to get some color on there). Sprinkle the chili powder on the beef along with some salt and pepper.

In a slow cooker, layer the onion, bell pepper, and beef. (If you're using a brisket, just put it in there whole. You'll shred it at the end.) Pour the Ro-Tel, salsa, and water over the top. Cover and cook on low for 7 to 8 hours or on high for 3 to 4 hours.

When you're ready to serve, remove the lid. If you're using a brisket, shred it right there inside your slow cooker using two forks. Scoop out a helping of the yummy beef mixture on top of a piece of cornbread. Garnish with your favorite toppings.

WEEK 4

SUN *Pepperoni Pizza Soup*

Make this soup the way you like it! You can make it in the slow cooker or on the stove, you can use any ground meat you like, and if you like other meats or veggies on your pizza, add them!

INGREDIENTS

1 pound ground beef

2 tablespoons Italian seasoning

Pinch ground fennel (optional)

1 onion, chopped

1 green bell pepper, chopped

1 (6 ounce) can tomato paste

1 (28 ounce) can crushed tomatoes

2 cups sliced pepperoni

1½ cups mozzarella cheese, shredded

Basil to garnish

1 can refrigerated biscuits

1 cup Parmesan cheese, grated

Slow cooker directions: In a skillet, brown ground beef; drain fat. Place the meat in a slow cooker and then add the next six ingredients. Cook on low 6 to 8 hours or on high 3 to 4 hours. When ready to serve, stir in pepperoni and garnish with mozzarella and basil. Serve with biscuits (see below).

Stovetop directions: In a large pot, cook ground beef over medium-high heat until brown and crumbly; drain fat. Stir in seasonings, onion, and bell pepper. Sauté a few minutes. Stir in tomato paste and crushed tomatoes. Reduce heat to low and simmer about 10 minutes. Break up the crushed tomatoes with a wooden spoon as you occasionally stir. Add in the pepperoni slices. Ladle soup into bowls and serve with mozzarella cheese and basil. Top with a biscuit.

To make biscuits, follow the directions on the can of biscuits. Before you place the biscuits in the oven, brush the tops with a little butter or olive oil and sprinkle Parmesan cheese on top. Bake according to package directions and serve.

Coconut Cream Pie

SWEET TREAT

Coconut Cream Pie is on every dessert table at every holiday party my family has. Maybe we see the fluffy coconut and it reminds us of snow? Maybe we're just so obsessed with coconut that we can't stand not to have it on one of the biggest days of the year? I toast my sweetened flaked coconut in a dry skillet, turning it continuously, for about five minutes.

INGREDIENTS

2 cups toasted coconut, divided

1½ cups half-and-half

1½ cups milk

2 eggs, lightly beaten

1 cup sugar

½ cup flour

1 teaspoon vanilla

1 (8 ounce) container whipped topping

1 homemade or store-bought pie crust baked in a 9-inch pie plate

In a saucepan over medium-high heat, bring the half-and-half, milk, eggs, sugar and flour to a boil, stirring constantly. Once the mixture boils, remove from heat and immediately stir in the vanilla and one cup of toasted coconut. Pour this filling into your baked pie shell.

Cover and chill at least 5 hours (I usually do it overnight).

Once chilled, combine your whipped topping and remaining cup toasted coconut (reserving just a little for garnish) and spread on top of your pie. Sprinkle a little more coconut on top. Cut and serve.

When not enjoying, store in the refrigerator.

Winter Notes

Index